COUNTDC

MATH

CW01481004

Jack Forster and Michael Wardle

Senior Lecturers in Mathematics Education
University of Warwick

Nelson

Thomas Nelson and Sons Ltd
Nelson House Mayfield Road
Walton-on-Thames Surrey
KT12 5PL UK

51 York Place
Edinburgh
EH1 3JD UK

Thomas Nelson (Hong Kong) Ltd
Toppan Building 10/F
22A Westlands Road
Quarry Bay Hong Kong

Thomas Nelson Australia
102 Dodds Street
South Melbourne
Victoria 3205 Australia

Nelson Canada
1120 Birchmount Road
Scarborough Ontario
M1K 5G4 Canada

First published by Macmillan Education Ltd 1978
ISBN 0-33342205-8

This edition published by Thomas Nelson and Sons Ltd 1992

ISBN 0-17-438549-8
NPN 9 8 7 6 5 4 3 2

Printed in England by Clays Ltd, St Ives plc

CONTENTS

Countdown to GCSE: Mathematics

ACKNOWLEDGEMENTS

The author and publishers wish to acknowledge the following source:

HMSO for extracts from The National Criteria, by permission of the Controller of Her Majesty's Stationery Office.
Dr Susan Pirie, for her compilation of the comparison of assessment patterns.

The publishers have made every effort to trace the copyright holders, but if they have inadvertently overlooked any, they will be pleased to make the necessary arrangements at the first opportunity.

SECTION I
Introduction — why GCSE?

If you have bought this book, it must be because you will be sitting the GCSE examination. GCSE stands for the 'General Certificate of Secondary Education'. The GCSE examination replaces the GCE 'O' level, CSE and 16+ exams.

Originally the GCE 'O' level examination was designed for the top 20% of the ability range. The CSE examination was then introduced to cater for the next 40% of the ability range. Many people, including students, parents and employers, found having two parallel examinations at sixteen confusing. Often this has led to difficult and sometimes quite arbitrary decisions being made about which particular exam students should take.

In addition, these examinations were administered by no fewer than twenty-two different exam boards, each setting its own syllabuses and exam papers, and people were concerned about the comparability between them.

As a result, some of the exam boards began to combine the GCE and CSE into a single common 16+ examination. Alongside this, changes began to take place within subject content, as old topics were replaced by new ones. Different forms of assessment began to be used in some areas, where coursework was allowed to contribute to the final mark as, for example, in the Mode 3 CSE exams. Also more emphasis was gradually placed on work in the classroom, on practical work, problem solving and investigations. All of this led to very wide variations, with students in different parts of the country following courses which sometimes had very little in common.

In June 1984, the Secretary of State for Education announced proposals for the new examination system, to be called the GCSE. The reasons for doing this were two-fold: firstly to introduce a common exam structure at first examination level, so that comparability could be achieved; secondly to introduce national criteria for each subject, so that all new syllabuses written would embody the same aims, and the forms of assessment used could be the most appropriate for each particular subject.

It is intended with GCSE that the grade achieved by a particular

1

student, in a particular subject, should more truly reflect his/her absolute knowledge of, and abilities within, that subject, rather than being pitched by comparison with other students.

GCE 'O' levels were graded A, B, C, D or E, and CSE passes were graded 1, 2, 3, 4, 5. A grade 1 pass in CSE was intended to be equivalent to at least a grade C pass in 'O' level. The table below shows how the seven new grades, A, B, C, D, E, F and G, for the GCSE examination roughly compare with the old grades for 'O' level and CSE.

'O' level	CSE	GCSE
A		A
B		B
C	1	C
D	2	D
E	3	E
	4	F
	5	G

The twenty-two different exam boards are now grouped into six larger examination associations — four in England, one in Northern Ireland and one in Wales. The new groups are often referred to by their initials:

NEA – Northern Examining Association;
MEG – Midland Examining Group;
SEG – Southern Examining Group;
LEAG – London and East Anglia Examining Group;
NISEC – Northern Ireland Schools Examinations Council;
WJEC – Welsh Joint Education Committee.

Each of these six associations/groups has the duty of producing its own syllabuses and methods of assessment. However, unlike in the previous situation, they now have to work within a framework agreed upon between all the exam boards, and approved by the Government.

This framework has been published in the form of *National Criteria*, which lay down minimum requirements for each syllabus in a particular subject, and give an indication of what students must achieve to be awarded a particular grade. The National Critera also lay down guidelines for the form of assessment to be used in each subject.

Whilst each of the six examination groups has to work within this agreed framework, there is still some flexibility, which will allow small variations to take place, both within the syllabuses, and also within the assessment procedures.

This book concentrates on the common features of all the mathematics syllabuses, and indicates the types of variations that may occur in these, and in the assessment procedures. It explains what is meant by the various terms used in the syllabus, and indicates the level which you are expected to reach to achieve particular grades. It also gives examples of typical exam papers, solutions to questions, and an indication of what the examiners will be looking for when awarding marks. The final section of the book is devoted to preparation for the exam itself during the lead-up and revision period.

SECTION 2
Mathematics: Aims and objectives; assessment

For many years there has been a great deal of discussion about the content of school mathematics courses. This really started in the early 1960s, after Russia sent the first Sputnik into orbit. As a result many people felt that the content of the mathematics syllabuses then taught in schools and colleges was no longer appropriate for the needs of the space age.

More recently, with the availability of cheap electronic calculators and small micro-computers, the syllabuses have again come under scrutiny to see whether certain traditionally taught numerical techniques, for example the use of logarithms, can still be justified.

In addition, following the setting up of a National Committee of Inquiry into the 'Teaching of Mathematics in Schools', a wide body of opinion was consulted about the real needs of business, commerce and industry, etc. and about how and where school mathematics matched or fell short of these requirements.

Under the chairmanship of Sir Wilfred Cockcroft, a very full report of the findings of this committee was published. The report covered not only the suggested content for mathematics syllabuses, but also, more importantly, it gave some indications of the types of mathematical activities which students should be engaged in during their course. These activities included such things as practical work, the use of maths as a means of solving practical problems, and also the experience of being involved in investigational work.

This type of work is necessary if students are going to be able to apply their knowledge to real situations, and if they are going to be able to think for themselves, rather than simply reproducing standard processes learnt by heart.

AIMS

The National Criteria for mathematics in the GCSE take fully into

4

account the findings of the Cockcroft Report and include the following list of ideal aims.

All courses should enable pupils to:

2.1 develop their mathematical knowledge and oral, written and practical skills in a manner which encourages confidence;

2.2 read about mathematics, and write and talk about the subject in a variety of ways;

2.3 develop a feel for number, carry out calculations and understand the significance of the results obtained;

2.4 apply mathematics in everyday situations and develop an understanding of the part which mathematics plays in the world around them;

2.5 solve problems, present the solutions clearly, check and interpret the results;

2.6 develop an understanding of mathematical principles;

2.7 recognise when and how a situation may be represented mathematically, identify and interpret relevant factors and, where necessary, select an appropriate mathematical method to solve the problem;

2.8 use mathematics as a means of communication with emphasis on the use of clear expression;

2.9 develop an ability to apply mathematics in other subjects, particularly science and technology;

2.10 develop the abilities to reason logically, to classify, to generalise and to prove;

2.11 appreciate patterns and relationships in mathematics;

2.12 produce and appreciate imaginative and creative work arising from mathematical ideas;

2.13 develop their mathematical abilities by considering problems and conducting individual and cooperative enquiry and experiment, including extended pieces of work of a practical and investigative kind;

2.14 appreciate the interdependence of different branches of mathematics;

2.15 acquire a foundation appropriate to their further study of mathematics and of other disciplines.

Stated baldly like this, the list looks pretty formidable, but in fact most of these aims are highly desirable if you are going to be able to make some use of your mathematics in later life. The examples below illustrate how some of these aims relate to everyday situations:

2.2 You should be able to look at a graph in a newspaper, or a graph of sales figures in an office, and obtain the correct information from it.

2.3 When buying (or selling) four shirts costing £7.99 each, you should be able to work out the cost quickly, without having to use a pencil and paper or a calculator (i.e., four at £8, less 4 p, which is £31.96)

2.4 It is useful to know that $9 \times 12 = 108$, but this will not help you unless you realise that this is the mathematics involved in finding the cost of 9 lb of plums costing 12 p a lb.

2.5 When you wish to redecorate a room, it is helpful to be able to work out how much wallpaper and paint you need, so that you do not buy more than you require.

2.8 Many people are confused when they see interest charges, or discounts, or pay rises quoted as percentages. Too often their use is not as clear and meaningful as it should be.

Now look again at aims *2.12* and *2.13*. These two aims illustrate one of the main differences between the old GCE and CSE, and the new GCSE examination. Neither of them can really be assessed by the formal written exam, so alternative forms of assessment have been introduced. Some exam groups include an oral or mental examination, as often occurs in languages such as French, together with one or more projects where you will be expected to explore and then write a report on some mathematical activity in which you have been involved.

OBJECTIVES

Whilst the National Criteria have indicated what they see as ideal aims for mathematics courses, they have also spelt out the 'Assessment Objectives' which each of the five examination groups is expected to use when designing its exams and awarding particular grades.

The following sets out the essential mathematical processes in which you will be assessed. As such, the objectives form a minimum list of qualities, abilities and skills.

Students should be able to:

3.1 recall, apply and interpret mathematical knowledge in the context of everyday situations;

3.2 set out mathematical work, including the solution of problems, in a logical and clear form using appropriate symbols and terminology;

3.3 organise, interpret and present information accurately in written, tabular, graphical and diagrammatic forms;

3.4 perform calculations by suitable methods;

3.5 use an electronic calculator;

3.6 understand systems of measurement in everyday use and make use of them in the solution of problems;

3.7 estimate, approximate and work to degrees of accuracy appropriate to the context;

3.8 use mathematical and other instruments to measure and to draw to an acceptable degree of accuracy;

3.9 recognise patterns and structures in a variety of situations, and form generalisations;

3.10 interpret, transform and make appropriate use of mathematical statements expressed in words or symbols;

3.11 recognise and use spatial relationships in two and three dimensions, particularly in solving problems;

3.12 analyse a problem, select a suitable strategy and apply an appropriate technique to obtain its solution;

3.13 apply combinations of mathematical skills and techniques in problem solving;

3.14 make logical deductions from given mathematical data;

3.15 respond to a problem relating to a relatively unstructured situation by translating it into an appropriately structured form.

Two further objectives have been included which necessitate a form of assessment, as indicated earlier, which is not the traditional written examination.

3.16 respond orally to questions about mathematics, discuss mathematical ideas and carry out mental calculations;

3.17 carry out practical and investigational work, and undertake extended pieces of work.

Section 3 looks at the actual content which is spelt out in the National Criteria and which forms the basis of the five exam groups' syllabuses. It shows how this content is related to the above objectives and gives examples of the level of work expected for three of the grades.

ASSESSMENT

In a subject like English, it is possible to set an exam question such as: 'Write an essay which starts with the line, "I was walking down a dark lane late at night and . . . " ' Every student is able to attempt this question, irrespective of his/her ability. More able students will produce more fluent and imaginative writing and so it is possible to use the full range of grades when marking a particular student's work.

However in mathematics, owing to the nature of the subject, it is very difficult to set questions in a written exam which all students can attempt. In algebra, for instance, the equations:

$$x + 3 = 5, 2x + 3 = 5, x^2 = 5 \text{ and } 2x^2 + 3x = 5$$

increase in difficulty from the first, which most students should be able to solve, to the last, which only a few would be able to attempt.

The National Criteria recognise this fact, and are insisting that the exam groups allow individual students to choose papers which enable them to demonstrate: 'what they know and can do rather than what they do not know and cannot do!'

As a result in mathematics, each exam group sets a number of exam papers of different degrees of difficulty and you are able to choose the ones which are the most appropriate for your ability. Your school (or college) will be able to advise you on this.

If you choose the easier paper(s), you will only be able to get one of the lower grades, say E, F or G. For the middle paper(s) you could get one of the middle grades, say C, D or E. But if you want a chance of getting one of the highest grades, i.e. A, B or C, then you will have to choose the hardest paper(s).

What is important is that you are entered for the paper(s) in which you can show your knowledge and ability. There is no point in being entered for the hardest paper(s) if you have no chance of answering the questions, since you are then likely not to be awarded any grade at all!

The scheme that most of the examination groups are using is illustrated below. There are four papers and each candidate has to choose one particular pair of papers.

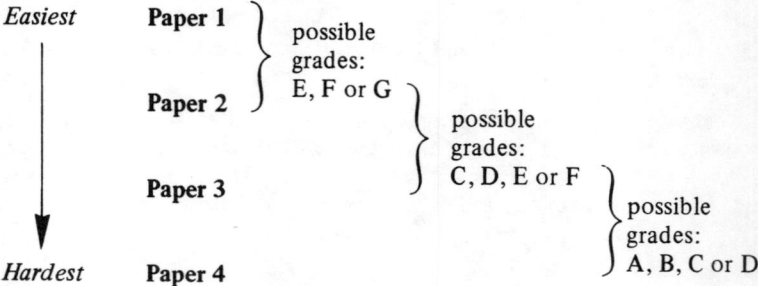

Easiest

Paper 1

Paper 2

possible grades: E, F or G

Paper 3

possible grades: C, D, E or F

Hardest **Paper 4**

possible grades: A, B, C or D

8

In this way, for most candidates, the choice of which pair of papers to select is not critical.

Clearly, in this scheme, less able candidates would be advised to select papers 1 and 2, whereas strong candidates would have to select papers 3 and 4 to have a chance of a high grade.

As a rough guide, candidates aiming at grades E, F and G, on the work focused at this general level, would be expected to score about 75% for a grade E, 65% for a grade F, and 50% for a grade G. Candidates aiming at grades C, D and E, on the work focused at this general level, would be expected to score about 75% for a grade C, 65% for a grade D, and 50% for a grade E. Candidates aiming at grades A, B and C, on the work focused at this general level, would be expected to score about 75% for a grade A, 65% for a grade B, and 50% for a grade C.

In addition, initially, all the exam groups must offer at least one scheme where a coursework element counting at least 20% of the marks is included. The National Criteria state that, from 1991 onwards, 'all schemes of assessment for mathematics must include a coursework element'. The coursework may take a variety of forms, including practical and investigational work. Again you will need to check with your school (or college) whether coursework is being included when you take your GCSE, and if so, precisely what form it will take.

A comparison of the patterns of assessment used by the different exam groups is included at the end of this book.

SECTION 3

Core syllabus in mathematics

In this section, we shall look in detail at the topics which you are expected to have covered in your syllabus.

The National Criteria state that the content of lists 1 and 2 below must be included in all mathematics syllabuses. If you are taking the exam which is aimed at Grades E, F and G, you will be expected to have covered all the topics which are in list 1. If you are taking the exam which is aimed at Grades C, D and E, you will be expected to have covered all the topics which are in list 1 and list 2, taken together. The content of lists 1 and 2 represent almost the whole of the syllabus for their respective examinations.

If you are taking the exam which is aimed at Grades A, B and C you will be expected to have covered all the topics which are in lists 1 and 2. These topics will account for between 50% and 70% of the marks. In addition you will be expected to have covered a number of other topics which will account for the remainder of the marks. These additional topics will depend on the particular syllabus your school or college has chosen to follow. Some of the most common additional topics are shown in list 3.

LIST 1

Whole numbers: odd, even, prime, square

You should recognise and know the names of:

counting numbers:	1, 2, 3, 4, 5, . . .
odd numbers:	1, 3, 5, 7, 9, . . .
even numbers:	2, 4, 6, 8, 10, . . .
prime numbers:	2, 3, 5, 7, 11, 13, . . .
square numbers	1, 4, 9, 16, 25, . . .

Note

A prime number is a number which has only itself and one as factors.
A square number is the number which is formed by multiplying a number by itself, e.g. 36, which is 6 × 6.

Factors, multiples, idea of square root

You should understand the meaning of, and be able to find:

factors:	6 has factors 1, 2, 3 and 6
	15 has factors 1, 3, 5 and 15
multiples:	3, 6, 9, 12, 15 are multiples of 3
	7, 14, 21 28, 35 are multiples of 7
square roots:	4 is the square root of 16
	9 is the square root of 81

Note

A factor of a number is any number, including itself or one, which will divide exactly into the number without leaving a remainder.

The square root of a number is the number which when multiplied by itself, gives the original number.

Directed numbers in practical situations

You should be able to recognise the directed numbers:

$$+ 1, -1, +2, -2, +3, -3 \ldots$$

and be able to relate them to everyday situations, such as positive and negative temperatures, heights above and below sea-level.

You should also be able to do simple calculations involving these ideas. For example:

How much does the temperature rise from $-12\,°C$ to $+23\,°C$?
(Here the rise in temperature is $35\,°C$.)

The number line
is a useful aid in this work.

$$-3 \quad -2 \quad -1 \quad 0 \quad 1 \quad 2 \quad 3$$

Vulgar and decimal fractions and percentages; equivalences between these forms in simple cases; conversion from vulgar to decimal fractions with the help of a calculator

Vulgar and decimal fractions

You should understand the meaning of fractions, such as:

$$\tfrac{1}{2}, \quad \tfrac{3}{4}, \quad 2\tfrac{1}{3}, \quad 1.5, \quad 0.8, \quad 3.14, \text{ etc.}$$

You should be able to show simple vulgar fractions as decimal fractions and vice-versa:

$$\tfrac{1}{2} = 0.5, \quad \tfrac{3}{4} = 0.75, \quad 0.8 = \tfrac{8}{10} = \tfrac{4}{5}, \quad \text{etc.}$$

For more complicated numbers, you will be expected to know how to use a calculator to do this:

$$\tfrac{7}{16} = 0.4375 \quad \text{by using} \boxed{7} \div \boxed{16} \boxed{=} \text{ on the calculator.}$$

11

Percentages

You should understand the meaning of percentages, such as:

5%, 20%, 75%, etc.

You should be able to convert these to fractions:

$5\% = \frac{5}{100} = \frac{1}{20}$, $20\% = \frac{20}{100} = \frac{1}{5}$, $75\% = \frac{75}{100} = \frac{3}{4}$, etc.

You should also be able to convert simple fractions to percentages:

$0.75 = \frac{75}{100} = 75\%$, $0.2 = \frac{2}{10} = \frac{20}{100} = 20\%$,

$\frac{3}{20} = \frac{3 \times 5}{20 \times 5} = \frac{15}{100} = 15\%$, etc.

Estimation and approximation to obtain reasonable answers

You should be able to estimate the answer to a calculation, so that you can check that the answer that you have obtained is a reasonable one. For example:

About how much would be the cost of 6 items, each costing £4.95? (An estimate for this would be: £5 × 6 = £30.)

The four rules applied to whole numbers and decimal fractions

You should be able to do calculations of the following types:

using whole numbers: 267 + 459, 1038 − 649, 312 × 23, 224 ÷ 7

using decimal fractions: 3.12 + 4.39, 61.7 − 43.8, 3.14 × 7, 6.21 ÷ 9

Language and notation of simple vulgar fractions in appropriate contexts, including addition and subtraction of vulgar (and mixed) fractions with simple denominators

You should understand how language such as 'two-fifths' can be represented in symbols $\frac{2}{5}$, and how vulgar fractions such as $\frac{7}{8}$ can be expressed in words.

You should also be able to add and subtract simple fractions. For example:

$\frac{3}{8} + \frac{7}{8} = 1\frac{2}{8} = 1\frac{1}{4}$, $2\frac{1}{4} - \frac{3}{8} = 1\frac{7}{8}$

Elementary ideas and notation of ratio

You should understand the meaning of a ratio, such as 1:3 or 2:5. You should be able to divide a number such as 28 in a given ratio. For example:

28 divided in the ratio 1:3 gives parts of 7 and 21.

Percentage of a sum of money

You should be able to find a percentage of a sum of money. For example:

$$5\% \text{ of } £80 \text{ is } \frac{5}{100} \times £80 = \frac{1}{20} \times £80 = £4$$

You should also be able to increase or decrease the sum of money by the given percentage, i.e. £80 + £4, or £80 − £4.

Scales, including map scales

You should understand the meaning of a scale, such as 1:10, when it is used on a drawing, e.g. 1 cm on the drawing represents 10 cm on the original.

You should be able to find the length which corresponds to a given distance on the drawing and vice-versa.

You should also understand how scales are used with maps. For example:

1:50 000 map means that 1 cm on the map represents 50 000 cm, or 500 m, or $\frac{1}{2}$ km on the ground.

Elementary ideas and applications of direct and inverse proportion

If two quantities are related so that when one of them is doubled or trebled, the other is also doubled or trebled, the two quantities are said to be in direct proportion. For example: when a car is travelling at a constant speed, if the distance travelled is doubled, then the time taken is also doubled. The distance and time are in direct proportion.

If two quantities are related so that when one of them is doubled, the other is halved, the two quantities are said to be in inverse proportion. For example: for a given distance, if the speed of a car is doubled, then the time taken is halved. The speed and time are in inverse proportion.

Common measures of rate

You should understand how to calculate and use common rates, such as kilometres per hour, miles per hour, miles per gallon, or kilometres per litre.

You should understand the idea of average speed, and be able to do simple calculations involving distance, speed and time.

Efficient use of an electronic calculator; application of appropriate checks of accuracy

You should be able to use an electronic calculator quickly and efficiently for addition, subtraction, multiplication and division, and possibly for finding square roots and reciprocals.

You should be able to check your results to make sure you haven't pressed a wrong key by mistake. Often the best way to do this is to repeat the calculation in a different order. For example:

3.17 + 2.68 + 5.97 can be checked by finding 5.97 + 2.68 + 3.17

Measures of weight, length, area, volume and capacity in current units

You should be familiar with using the following units.

Mass

kilograms (kg)			pounds (lb)	
grams (g)	1000 g	= 1 kg	ounces (oz)	16 oz = 1 lb

Length

kilometres (km)			miles (M)	
metres (m)	1000 m	= 1 km	yards (yd)	
centimetres (cm)	100 cm	= 1 m	feet (ft)	3 ft = 1 yd
millimetres (mm)	10 mm	= 1 cm	inches (in)	12 in = 1 ft

Area

hectares (ha)		
square metres (m²)	$10000\,m^2$	= 1 ha
square centimetres (cm²)	$10000\,cm^2$	= 1 m²
square millimetres (mm²)	$100\,mm^2$	= 1 cm²

Volume

cubic metres (m³)		
cubic centimetres (cm³)	$1\,000\,000\,cm^3$	= 1 m³
cubic millimetres (mm³)	$1000\,mm^3$	= 1 cm³

Capacity

litres (l)	gallons	8 pints = 1 gallon
centilitres (cl)	pints	
millilitres (ml)		

Note

1 cubic centimetre (cm³) is the same as 1 millilitre (ml).
1000 cubic centimetres is the same as 1 litre.
1 cubic centimetre of water has a mass of 1 gram.

Time: 24-hour and 12-hour clock

You should understand times given in both the 12-hour clock system and in the 24-hour clock system, and be able to convert one to the other. For example:

2315 is the same as 11.15 p.m.

You should also be able to find the times of journeys when given the start and finish times, or to calculate lengths of time from timetables.

For example:

The time between 9.30 a.m. and 2.10 p.m. is 4 hours and 40 minutes.

Money, including the use of foreign currencies

You will be expected to carry out simple calculations involving money, and to convert amounts from one currency to another when given the exchange rate. For example:

If £1 = $1.42, how many dollars would I get for £70?

Personal and household finance, including hire-purchase, interest, taxation, discount, loans, wages and salaries

You will be expected to understand commonly used terms, such as:

A 10% discount is given for cash payments.
The interest charged on a bank loan is 19% per annum.
After taking off allowances of £2500, the remainder of his salary is taxed at 29%.

Profit and loss, VAT

You will be expected to carry out calculations involving percentage profit or loss, and know how to find the VAT to add to the cost of an article. For example:

A man buys a car for £2000. When he sells it he makes a 7% loss. For what price did he sell the car?
(The loss is 7% of £2000 = £140, so he sold the car for £1860.)

Reading of clocks and dials

You should be able to read both the 12-hour and 24-hour clock, and also meters with dials, such as those used for electricity or gas. For example:

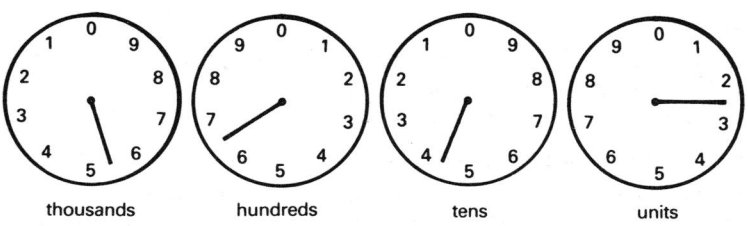

| thousands | hundreds | tens | units |

Use of tables and charts

You should be able to extract information from timetables or charts, and also be able to use ready reckoners for simple calculations.

Mathematical language used in the media

You should be able to understand information presented in newspapers and advertisements, and in particular when graphs or percentages are used. You should also be aware when these have been used in a misleading or incorrect way.

Simple change of units including foreign currency

You should be able to change from one set of units to another, for example, from cm to mm or m, and also from one currency to another when you are given the exchange rate.

Average speed

You should understand the idea of average speed and be able to find the average speed for a journey, by dividing the distance travelled by the time taken.

Cartesian coordinates

You should understand how coordinates such as (5, 3) can be used to represent a point on a graph. You will be expected to be able to plot points with given coordinates, and to write down the coordinates of a given point.

Interpretation and use of graphs in practical situations including travel graphs and conversion graphs

You should be able to interpret the information given in a graph such as a travel graph, and to use a graph such as a conversion graph to change one quantity into another.

Drawing graphs from given data

You will be expected to be able to draw a graph from given data. The data might be in the form of a table showing the distance travelled for given times.

The use of letters for generalised numbers

You should understand how letters can be used to represent numbers in a formula, such as $V = lbh$, or $A = \frac{1}{2} bh$.

Substitution of numbers for words and letters in formulae

You should be able to use a formula, like the one above to find the value of V when the values of l, b and h are given. You should also be able to use a formula when the connection between the quantities is given in words. For example:

The tax payable is found by taking 29% of the balance left when the allowances are deducted from the man's pay.

The geometrical terms: point, line, parallel, right angle, acute and obtuse angles, perpendicular

You should understand the idea of a point, and a line which is made up of a set of points.

You should be able to recognise when two lines are parallel or perpendicular, and when an angle is a right angle, an acute angle or an obtuse angle.

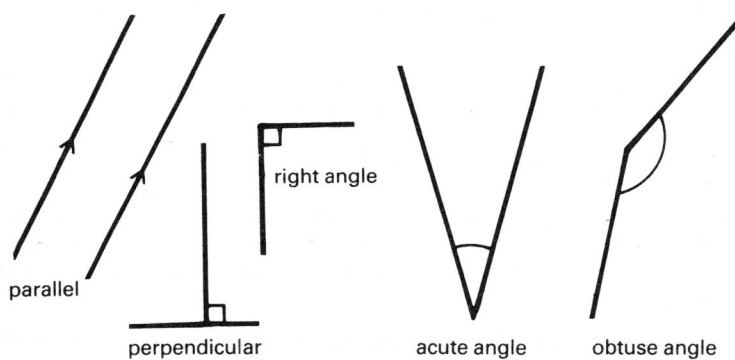

Bearings

You should understand how an angle between 0° and 360°, measured from a north line, can be used as a bearing.

Similarity

You should understand the idea of similar figures, i.e. figures such as enlargements of photographs, which look alike but which are of different size.

Note

The corresponding angles in similar figures are the same size, and the lengths of the corresponding sides are in the same ratio.

Measurement of lines and angles

You should be able to measure the length of a line with a ruler, and the size of an angle with a protractor, each to a reasonable degree of accuracy.

Angles at a point

You should know that the angle on a straight line is 180°, and that the sum of the angles at a point is 360°.

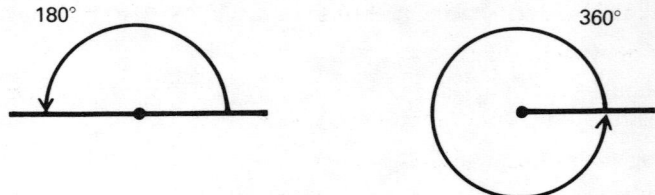

Enlargement

You should understand the idea of an enlargement and its associated scale factor. You should also know how to enlarge a figure with a given scale factor.

Vocabulary of triangles, quadrilaterals and circles; properties of these figures directly related to their symmetries

You should know the meaning of the words:

   equilateral, isosceles, scalene, right-angled, acute-angled and obtuse-angled, for triangles;
   square and rectangle, for quadrilaterals;
   centre, radius, diameter, circumference and π, for circles.

You should be able to identify the properties of the angles and sides, of the above triangles and quadrilaterals, and also the symmetries of these figures.

Angle properties of triangles and quadrilaterals

You should know that the angle sum of any triangle is 180°, and that the angle sum of any quadrilateral is 360°.

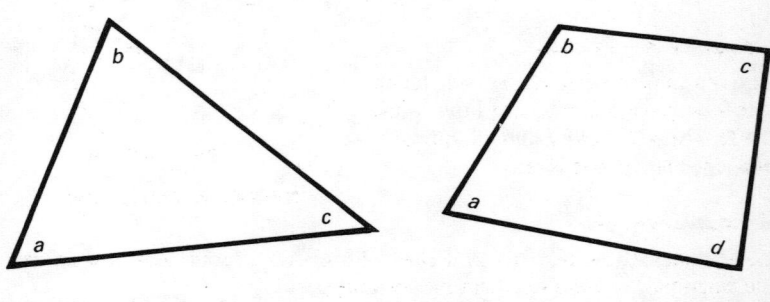

$$a + b + c = 180°$$

$$a + b + c + d = 360°$$

Simple solid figures

You should be able to recognise a cube, a cuboid, a cylinder and a sphere, and be able to identify their faces, edges and vertices if any.

Use of drawing instruments

You should be able to use a ruler, a protractor and a pair of compasses, to construct and measure lengths and angles.

Reading and making of scale drawings

You should be able to use the above instruments to make simple scale drawings, and to read lengths and angles off these drawings.

Perimeter and area of rectangle and triangle

You should know how to find the perimeter and area of a rectangle and a triangle, and how to use the formulae:

$$p = 2(l + b); A = lb; p = a + b + c \text{ and } A = \tfrac{1}{2} bh.$$

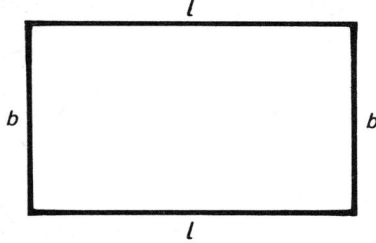

perimeter $p = 2(l + b)$
area $\quad A = lb$

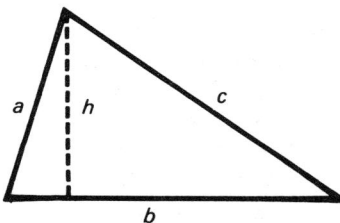

perimeter $p = a + b + c$
area $\quad A = \tfrac{1}{2} bh$

Circumference of circle

You should know how to find the circumference of a circle, and how to use the formula $C = 2\pi r$ when an appropriate value for π is given.

circumference $C = 2\pi r$

Volume of cuboid

You should know how to find the volume of a cuboid, and how to use the formula $V = lbh$ (see diagram on next page).

You should also know how to find the surface area of a cuboid.

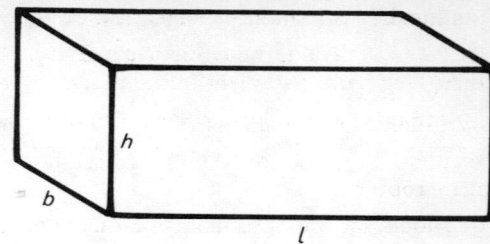

volume	$V = lbh$
surface area	$A = 2lh + 2bh + 2lb$

Collection, classification and tabulation of statistical data

You should be able to collect, classify and tabulate statistical data from a simple survey.

Reading, interpreting and drawing simple inferences from tables and statistical diagrams

You should be able to read, interpret and draw simple conclusions from statistical tables, bar charts, pie charts and pictograms.

Construction of bar charts and pictograms

You should be able to construct bar charts and pictograms from simple statistical data.

Measures of average and the purpose for which they are used

You should know how to find the mean, mode and median of a given population.

You should also know what the differences between these 'averages' are, and the purpose for which each might be used.

Probability involving only one event

You should understand the idea of the probability of an event occurring, as a measure of how likely, or not, it is to happen. You should understand the idea of equally likely events, and be able to find probabilities in simple cases involving a single event only, such as rolling a die, or picking a coloured bead from a bag of differently coloured beads.

LIST 2

Natural numbers, integers, rational and irrational numbers

You should understand that there are different types of numbers:

    naturals: 1,   2,   3,   4,   5 . . . etc.
    integers: ±1, ±2, ±3, ±4 . . . etc.

rationals: any number which can be shown as a vulgar fraction, or as a terminating decimal, e.g. $\frac{2}{3}$, $\frac{5}{8}$, $\frac{25}{12}$, 0.27, 1.5, etc;

irrationals: any number which cannot be shown as a vulgar fraction, e.g. π, $\sqrt{2}$, etc.

Square roots

You should be able to obtain an estimate for the square root of a number. You should also be able to find the square root both by using tables, and by using a calculator.

Common factors, common multiples

You should be able to find the common factors, and highest common factor, and also the common multiples, and lowest common multiple, of two or more numbers. For example:

1, 2, 4 and 8 are the common factors of 16 and 24,
so 8 is the HCF of 16 and 24.
48, 96, 144 are the common multiples of both 16 and 24,
so 48 is the LCM of 16 and 24.

Conversion between vulgar and decimal fractions and percentages

You should be able to convert a number, given as a vulgar fraction, into a decimal fraction, or into a percentage and vice-versa.

Standard form

You should understand what is meant by, and be able to express a given number in, standard form. For example:

$127.5 = 1.275 \times 10^2$: $8.6 \times 10^4 = 86\,000$

Approximation to a given number of significant figures or decimal places

You should be able to give your answers to a calculation, and rewrite specified numbers, correct to a given number of significant figures, or to a given number of decimal places. For example:

1.275 is 1.3 correct to two significant figures, or 1.28 correct to two decimal places.

(Remember if the next figure is 5 or more then the previous figure is rounded up.)

Appropriate limits of accuracy

You should be aware of what a reasonable answer is for a particular calculation. When, for instance, you are using approximate measurements in a calculation, it is unreasonable to give the answers to a greater degree of accuracy than that used for the original data. This is particularly important when using a calculator, as often up to eight decimal places are displayed.

The four rules applied to vulgar (and mixed) fractions

You will be expected to carry out calculations involving addition, subtraction, multiplication and division, with both vulgar and mixed fractions, as well as ones involving whole numbers or decimal fractions.

Expression of one quantity as a percentage of another

You should be able to express one number as a percentage of another. For example:

Express 7 as a percentage of 40.

$$\frac{7}{40} = \frac{7 \times 2.5}{40 \times 2.5} = \frac{17.5}{100} = 17.5\%$$

Percentage change

You should be able to express the change in some quantity as a percentage of that quantity. For example:

Find the percentage change when a volume increases from $40\,cm^3$ to $43\,cm^3$.

The change is $3\ cm^3$, so the percentage change is given by:

$$\frac{3}{40} = \frac{3 \times 2.5}{40 \times 2.5} = \frac{7.5}{100} = 7.5\%$$

Proportional division

You should know how to divide a given quantity into given proportions, such as $1:3:4$. For example:

72 divided in the proportions $1:3:4$ is $9, 27$ and 36.

Constructing tables for given functions which include expressions of the form: $ax + b$, ax^2, a/x $(x \neq 0)$ where a and b are integral constants

You should be able to construct a table of values for functions such as:

$y = 2x + 3$, $y = 3x^2$ and $y = \frac{4}{x}$.

Drawing and interpretation of related graphs; idea of gradient

You should be able to draw graphs for functions like the ones above, using the table of values.

You should be able to recognise lines such as $y = x$, $y = 3$ and $x = 5$, and be able to identify regions bounded by these lines.

You should be able to find the gradient of a straight line, both directly from the graph, and also from the equation.

Note

In the equation $y = 5x + 2$, the 5 is the gradient of the line, and the 2 is the value of y where the line crosses the y-axis.

Transformation of simple formulae

You should be able to rearrange a simple formula so that a different letter is made the subject. For example:

The formulae $V = lbh$ can be rewritten as $h = \dfrac{V}{lb}$ and

$v = u + at$ can be rewritten as $t = \dfrac{v - u}{a}$.

Basic arithmetic processes expressed algebraically

You should understand how $a + a + a$ can be written as $3a$, whereas $a \times a \times a$ is written as a^3, and be able to collect together like terms to simplify algebraic expressions.

Directed numbers

You will be expected to carry out simple calculations involving the addition, subtraction, multiplication and division of both positive and negative numbers.

Use of brackets and extraction of common factors

You will be expected to be able to rewrite expressions such as $6x - 8y$ as $2(3x - 4y)$ by taking out common factors and using brackets.

You will also be expected to be able to simplify algebraic expressions by first removing any brackets.

Positive and negative integral indices

You should understand the meaning and use of both positive and negative indices. For example:

$$2^3 = 8, \quad 3^{-2} = \frac{1}{3^2} = \frac{1}{9}, \quad a^5, \quad a^{-5} = \frac{1}{a^5}, \text{etc.}$$

You should also be able to simplify expressions such as:

$2^3 \times 2^4, \quad a^5 \times a^3$.

Simple linear equations in one unknown

You should be able to solve linear equations, such as:

$$3x + 5 = 17, 4 - x = 9, \text{and } \frac{x}{2} - 3 = 5.$$

Congruence

You should understand the idea of congruence when applied to geometric shapes, i.e. two shapes are said to be congruent if they are identical.

Angles formed within parallel lines

You should be able to identify alternate, corresponding and vertically opposite angles.

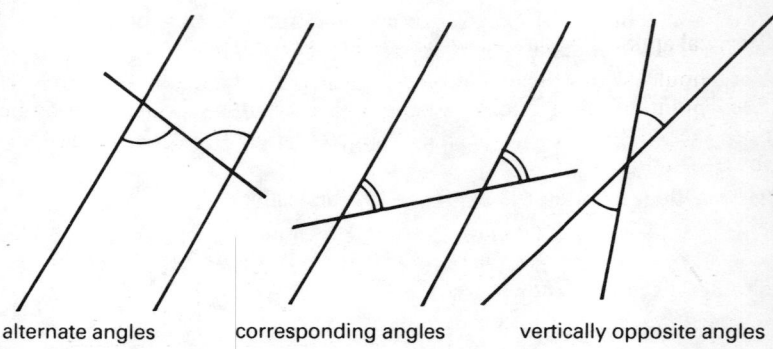

alternate angles   corresponding angles   vertically opposite angles

Properties of polygons directly related to their symmetries

You should be able to recognise a regular polygon, i.e. one which has all its angles the same size and all its edges the same length, and be able to identify pentagons, hexagons and octagons.

You should be able to identify the symmetries of regular polygons and also those of parallelograms, rhombuses and trapezia.

Angle in a semi-circle; angle between the tangent and radius of a circle

You should be familiar with the words: chord, arc, tangent and sector, when applied to a circle.

You should know that the angle formed in a semi-circle, and between the radius and tangent of a circle, are both right angles.

You should also know that the perpendicular bisector of a chord passes through the centre of the circle.

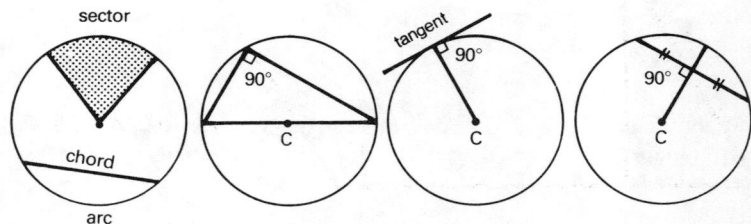

Angle properties of regular polygons

You should know how to find the angle in a given regular polygon. You should also know that the sum of the exterior angles of any polygon is always $360°$, and that the sum of the interior angles is $(2n - 4)$ right angles.

Practical applications based on simple locus properties

You should know that the points which are a fixed distance from a fixed point lie on a circle, and the points which are equidistant from two fixed points lie on the perpendicular bisector of the line joining those two points.

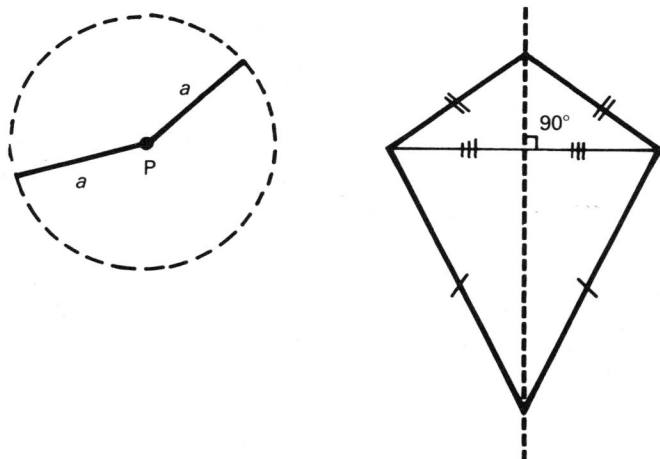

Area of parallelogram

You should know that the area of a parallelogram is found by multiplying the length of one side by the perpendicular distance between that side and the opposite side.

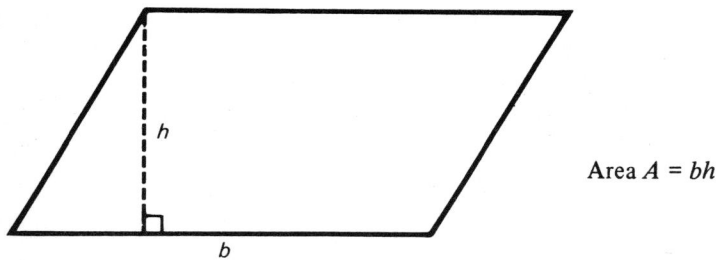

Area $A = bh$

25

Area of circle

You should be able to find the area of a circle by using the formula $A = \pi r^2$.

Volume of cylinder

You should be able to find the volume of a cylinder by using the formula $V = \pi r^2 h$, or by multiplying the cross-sectional area of the cylinder by its length.

You should also be able to recognise a prism, pyramid and cone, and be able to draw a net for a cuboid or simple prism.

volume $V = \pi r^2 h$
  or $V = Ah$

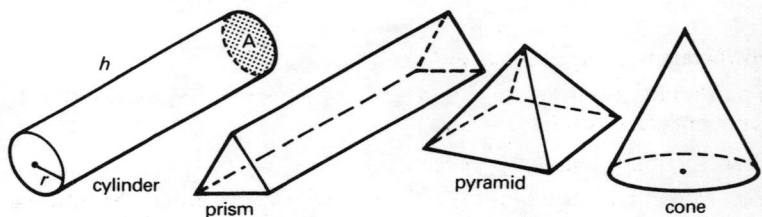

cylinder
prism
pyramid
cone

Results of Pythagoras

You should know how to use Pythagoras' theorem to find the length of a side of a right-angled triangle.

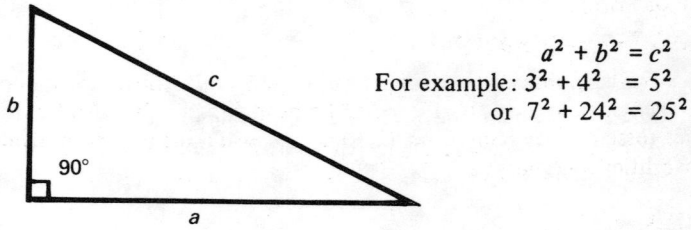

$$a^2 + b^2 = c^2$$
For example: $3^2 + 4^2 = 5^2$
  or $7^2 + 24^2 = 25^2$

Sine, cosine and tangent for acute angles

You should know how to find the sine, cosine or tangent of an angle given in degrees (e.g. $\sin 23.6°$), and also how to find the angle for a given sine, cosine or tangent.

Application of these to the calculation of a side or an angle of a right-angled triangle

You should be able to use sines, cosines and tangents to find an unknown length or angle in a right-angled triangle.

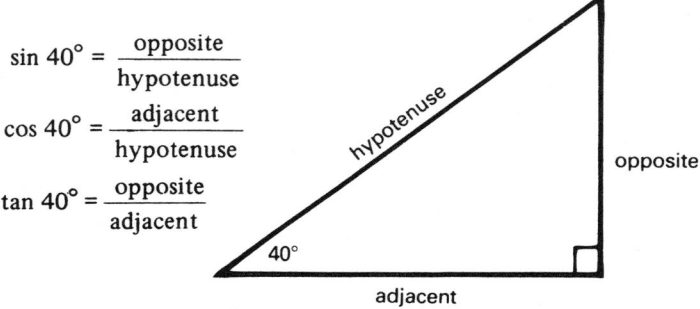

$$\sin 40° = \frac{\text{opposite}}{\text{hypotenuse}}$$

$$\cos 40° = \frac{\text{adjacent}}{\text{hypotenuse}}$$

$$\tan 40° = \frac{\text{opposite}}{\text{adjacent}}$$

Histogram with equal intervals

You should understand how to draw a histogram with equal intervals to represent statistical information.

Construction and use of pie charts

You should be able to construct a pie chart, and interpret the information shown in a given pie chart.

Construction and use of simple frequency distributions

You should be able to construct a frequency distribution table, to show how often certain events happen, and to use this to draw a frequency graph or histogram.

Simple combined probabilities

You should be able to find simple combined probabilities for independent events, such as getting 'a six and a head' when a die is rolled and a coin is tossed at the same time. (In this case you multiply the individual probabilities together, i.e. $\frac{1}{6} \times \frac{1}{2} = \frac{1}{12}$.)

LIST 3

Each examining group has the freedom to include whatever topics it feels are appropriate for extension material in its own syllabus. The topics which follow are a selection of the more common areas of work which are included in the syllabuses for those candidates aiming at grades A, B or C.

If you are aiming at one of these higher grades, you will be expected to cover most of these topics, in addition to those already mentioned in lists 1 and 2. You will need to check with your school or college to find out exactly what additional topics are included in your particular syllabus.

Powers, roots and reciprocals

You will be expected to be able to work with both negative and fractional indices, and to use these with either tables or calculators to find roots and reciprocals.

You should also be familiar with the laws of indices:

$$a^m a^n = a^{m+n}, \ \frac{a^m}{a^n} = a^{m-n}, (a^m)^n = a^{mn}, \ a^{-n} = \frac{1}{a^n} \text{ and } a^0 = 1.$$

Sets, language and notation

You should be familiar with the idea of the universal set, union, intersection, complement, subset, empty set, the number of elements in a set and disjoint sets, and also the notation:

$$\cup, \cap, ', \subset, \phi \text{ and } n\ (\ ).$$

You should be able to use Venn diagrams to help you to solve problems involving two or three different sets.

Functions

You should be familiar with the idea of a function, its domain and range, and the notation:

$$y = 2x + 3, \quad f(x) = 2x + 3 \text{ or } \quad f: x \mapsto 2x + 3.$$

You should be able to use a table of values to help you to draw the graph of a given function, including the quadratic $f(x) = ax^2 + bx + c$, where a, b and c are constants.

Gradient

You will be expected to be able to find the gradient of a line, both from its graph and its equation $y = mx + c$, and also the gradient of a curve at a point, by drawing the tangent to the curve at that point.

Formulae

You will be expected to be able to construct and to interpret formulae, expressed either in words or in letters, and also to be able to change the subject of a formula.

Factorisation

You should be able to expand products of the form $(ax + by)(cx + dy)$ and $(ax + by)^2$, and to factorise expressions including those of the form $ax^2 + bx + c$.

You should know and be able to apply the results:
$(a + b)^2 = a^2 + 2ab + b^2$, $(a - b)^2 = a^2 - 2ab + b^2$, and also that for the difference of two squares: $a^2 - b^2 = (a + b)(a - b)$.

Equations and inequalities

You will be expected to be able to manipulate, and solve, linear equations and linear inequalities in one unknown, including those which involve fractions.

Simultaneous equations

You will be expected to be able to solve simultaneous equations by both graphical and algebraic methods. You should also be able to identify regions on a graph described by simultaneous inequalities.

Quadratic equations

You should understand the idea that if $xy = 0$ then either $x = 0$ or $y = 0$, and you will be expected to be able to solve quadratic equations by factorisation, or by using the formula which will be given.

Direct and inverse variation

You should understand the idea of direct variation ($y \propto x$) and inverse variation ($y \propto \frac{1}{x}$), and be able to find the constants of variation.

Transformations

You should be familiar with the transformations of reflection, rotation, translation and enlargement, and the idea of axes and planes of symmetry.

You should be able to use the idea of a column vector $\begin{pmatrix} a \\ b \end{pmatrix}$ to describe a translation, and understand how to find a mirror line in a reflection and the centre and angle of rotation.

You should understand how to use both positive and negative scale factors for enlargements, and know how these affect area and volume.

You should be able to combine two or more of the above transformations, and show the result of using them in different orders.

Angle properties of a circle

You should be familiar with the following angle properties of a circle:

The angle at the centre is twice the angle on the circumference.
The angles in the same segment are equal.
The sum of the opposite angles of a cyclic quadrilateral is $180°$.

Mensuration

You should be familiar with the properties of a trapezium and know how to find its area.

You should be familiar with the properties of, and be able to find the surface area and volume of, a prism, a sphere, a pyramid and a cone. You should also know how to draw nets for prisms and pyramids.

Ratio of areas and volumes of similar shapes

You should know that the ratio of the areas of similar shapes is equal to the ratio of the squares of their corresponding sides, and that the ratio of the volumes of similar shapes is equal to the ratio of the cubes of their corresponding sides.

Sectors and segments

You should be able to find the length of an arc, and the area of a sector and a segment, of a circle.

Trigonometry

You should be able to apply the use of sines, cosines and tangents, and also Pythagoras' theorem, to problems in both two and three dimensions.

Probability

You should be familiar with the ideas of both independent and dependent events, and be able to use tree diagrams to find probabilities of combined events.

Matrices

You should understand the ideas of the identity matrix, multiplication by a scalar, matrix multiplication and the inverse of a matrix.

You should know how to represent the transformations of reflection, rotation and enlargement, using matrices, and be able to combine them.

Vectors

You should understand how a vector can be used to represent a position vector, or a translation.

You should be able to add two column vectors, and to find the magnitude and direction of a vector.

You should be able to apply vectors to simple geometrical situations.

GRADE DESCRIPTIONS

The National Criteria provide the following general indication of the standards of achievement likely to have been shown by candidates who have been awarded particular grades.

A grade F candidate is likely to have shown a good knowledge of the subject content contained in list 1 and would be familiar with the associated processes and skills. He should be able to apply this knowledge to problems which involve a single idea or concept. The problems are likely to be of the type that the candidate has met before.

A grade C candidate is likely to have shown a good knowledge of the subject content contained in both lists 1 and 2, and would be able to execute accurately the processes and skills associated with the content in list 1. He should be able to apply the knowledge, processes and skills to structured situations, and show an ability to select a correct strategy to solve a problem which contains a number of ideas or concepts.

A grade A candidate is likely to have shown a good knowledge of the subject content contained in lists 1 and 2, and the appropriate parts of list 3 (or its equivalent), and would be able to execute accurately the processes and skills associated with the content in lists 1 and 2. He should be able to demonstrate powers of abstraction, generalisation and proof, and also his ability to continue the study of mathematics to higher level.

Section 2 included a list of the National Criteria's Assessment Objectives which each of the exam groups is expected to use when designing its examinations. The National Criteria also give an indication of how these objectives should be interpreted when awarding particular grades.

The examples which follow show, for a particular objective, the difference in the level which might be expected from a grade F, a grade C and a grade A candidate.

3.3   organise, interpret and present information accurately in written, tabular, graphical and diagrammatic forms;

Grade F: Draw a bar chart. Plot given points. Read a travel graph.

Grade C: Construct a pie chart. Plot the graph of a linear function.

Grade A: Make quantitative and qualitative deductions from distance–time and velocity–time graphs.

3.4   perform calculations by suitable methods;

Grade F: Add and subtract money and simple fractions. Calculate a simple percentage of a given sum of money.

Grade C: Apply the four rules to vulgar and decimal fractions. Calculate percentage change.

Grade A: Relate a percentage change to a multiplying factor and vice versa, e.g. multiplication by 1.05 results in a 5% increase.

3.5 **use an electronic calculator;**

Grade F: Perform calculations involving one operation only.

Grade C: Perform calculations involving several operations, including negative numbers.

Grade A: Perform calculations involving positive, negative and fractional indices.

3.6 **understand systems of measurement in everyday use and make use of them in the solution of problems;**

Grade F: Measure length, weight and capacity using metric units.

Grade C: Use area and volume units.

Grade A: Find surface areas and volumes of different solids.

3.7 **estimate, approximate and work to degrees of accuracy appropriate to the context;**

Grade F: Perform a money calculation with a calculator and express the answer to the nearest penny.

Grade C: Give a reasonable approximation to a calculator calculation involving the four rules.

Grade A: Express the result of a calculation to 1, 2 or 3 significant figures.

3.8 **use mathematical and other instruments to measure and to draw to an acceptable degree of accuracy;**

Grade F: Draw a triangle given the three sides. Measure a given angle.

Grade C: Use a scale drawing to solve a two-dimensional problem.

Grade A: Use a scale model to calculate actual lengths, areas and volumes.

3.9 **recognise patterns and structures in a variety of situations, and form generalisations;**

Grade F: Continue a straightforward pattern or number sequence.

Grade C: Recognise, and in simple cases formulate, rules for generating a pattern or sequence.

Grade A: Write down algebraic formulae and equations to describe situations or generalisations.

3.10 **interpret, transform and make appropriate use of mathematical statements expressed in words or symbols;**

Grade F: Use simple formulae, e.g. gross wage = wage per hour × number of hours worked, and use of $A = l \times b$ to find the area of a rectangle.

Grade C: Solve simple linear equations. Transform simple formulae. Substitute numbers into a formula and evaluate the remaining term.

Grade A: Manipulate algebraic equations and remove and insert brackets in algebraic expressions.

3.11 **recognise and use spatial relationships in two and three dimensions, particularly in solving problems;**

Grade F: Find the perimeter and area of a rectangle. Find the volume of a cuboid.

Grade C: Calculate the length of the third side of a right-angled triangle. Find the angle in a right-angled triangle, given two sides.

Grade A: Carry out calculations involving the use of right-angled triangles as part of work in three dimensions.

The next section looks at some of the possible forms of school-based assessment. When this is used, it will again be related to the content of lists 1, 2 and 3 for the particular target grades. Examples of oral questions corresponding to each of grades F, C and A further illustrate the differences in the expectations of attainment for each of these grades.

SECTION 4
School-based assessment in mathematics

Two of the objectives which are contained in the National Criteria necessitate a form of assessment which cannot be carried out using the traditional timed examination. These are to:

3.16 **respond orally to questions about mathematics, discuss mathematical ideas and carry out mental calculations;**

3.17 **carry out practical and investigational work, and undertake extended pieces of work.**

Both of these objectives require some form of school-based assessment. The first is likely to involve an oral and/or aural test, whilst the second necessitates some form of coursework.

Initially, all the examination groups are having to offer at least one scheme where a coursework element counting for at least 20% of the marks is included. If your school is not yet using this scheme, you will be assessed entirely by written examinations.

From 1991 onwards, the National Criteria have stated that 'all schemes of assessment for mathematics must include a coursework element'. From that time the coursework element will be at least 20% of the total assessment and can be as much as 50%. Since, within these broad guidelines, each of the examination groups has the freedom to devise its own assessment scheme, you will need to find out from your school exactly what form your coursework will take.

This section looks at the types of aural test and coursework that are likely to be used, but it should be realised that the actual form of these, and the relative weighting between them, differ quite widely between the various examination groups. A comparison of these differences is included on pages 98–101.

AURAL TESTS

When an oral test or tests are included, they are likely to correspond to the exam papers that you are taking. It is likely that you will be doing

34

the one which is designed for your target grade. If you are aiming at a high grade, the questions you are expected to answer will be more difficult than if you are aiming at a lower grade.

The examples of oral questions which follow are intended to illustrate the differences between the levels required for grades F, C and A. Each question would be read to you, and you would be expected to answer the question and write down the answer in about fifteen seconds.

Question 1
F: What is the cost of eight jackets at twenty pounds each?
C: What is the cost of eight note-pads at forty-five pence each?
A: What is the cost of eight drinks at ninety-nine pence each?

Question 2
F: I bought twelve cards for a total cost of ninety-six pence. How much each were they?
C: I bought twenty-five cans of Coke for a total cost of ten pounds. How much each were they?
A: I bought eight cups of coffee for a total of two pounds and eighty-eight pence. How much each were they?

Question 3
F: If you spend seventy-three pence and pay with a pound coin, how much change should you get?
C: My family eats two-thirds of a sponge cake every day. How many cakes will they eat in one week?
A: I bought a car radio marked at thirty pounds plus VAT at fifteen per cent. How much VAT did I pay?

Question 4
F: I bought a cup of tea and a chocolate bar for a total of forty-two pence. The cup of tea cost me twenty-five pence. How much was the chocolate bar?
C: My antique clock was made in eighteen hundred and twenty. How long ago was that?
A: My uncle is eighty-nine this year. Write down the year in which he was born.

Question 5
F: I arrived at the race twenty minutes before it started. My friend was five minutes late. How long was I there before my friend arrived?
C: I arrived at the race twenty-three minutes before it started. My friend arrived nine minutes before it started. How long had I been there when my friend arrived?
A: When I put some vegetables into my deep-freeze, the temperature

was nine degrees Celsius. When I came to take them out four hours later, the temperature was minus five degrees Celsius. How much did the temperature fall in this time?

Question 6
F: It takes me eight minutes to cycle two miles. If I do not alter my speed, how much longer will it take me to cycle a further four miles?

C: It takes me thirty minutes to cycle to see my aunt. I can drive there three times as fast. How long does it take me when I drive?

A: It takes me twenty minutes to drive sixteen miles on a motorway. If I do not alter my speed, how long will it take me to drive forty miles?

Question 7
F: Write down the approximate value of the total cost of four shirts at seven pounds ninety-nine pence each.

C: Write down an approximate value for fifty-nine times thirty-one.

A: Write down the approximate value of the total cost of three hundred and twenty plugs at sixty-eight pence each.

Question 8
F: A room measures six metres by four metres. What is the area of the room?

C: The diameter of a circle is four metres. Approximately what is its circumference?

A: The circumference of a circle is twenty-four metres. Approximately what is its radius?

Question 9
F: Estimate in degrees the size of the angle shown.

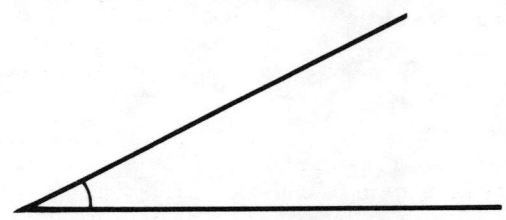

C: Estimate in degrees the size of the angle shown.

36

A: Estimate in degrees the size of the angle shown.

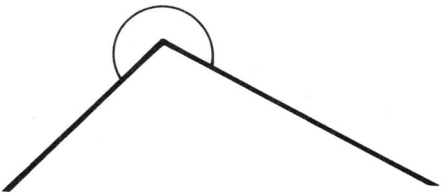

Question 10
F: The rectangle is drawn to scale. Estimate in centimetres the length of the rectangle.

4cm

C: The rectangle is drawn to scale. The length of the longer side is six centimetres. Estimate in centimetres the length of the shorter side.

A: The rectangle is drawn to scale. The length of the shorter side is four centimetres. Estimate in square centimetres the area of the rectangle.

Question 11

F:	Look at the cinema programme. How long does the main film last?	Cartoon	1715
C:	Look at the cinema programme. How long does the full programme last?	Intermission	1745
		Main film	1805
		Intermission	1940
		Cartoon	2010
A:	Look at the cinema programme. How long is it from the end of the cartoon to the beginning of the next showing of the cartoon?	Intermission	2040
		Main film	2100
		Doors close	2245

37

Question 12

F: The cost of an excursion is given in the table shown on the right. What is the cost for a twelve-year old?

C: The cost of an excursion is given in the table shown on the right. What is the cost for two adults, one child of six, and one child of two?

A: The cost of an excursion is given in the table shown on the right. What is the cost for three adults and three children of nine?

DAY EXCURSION RATES	
Adults	£2.50
Children (11–16)	£1.50
Children (7–11)	£0.75
Children (3–7)	£0.50
Children under 3	free
O.A.P.s	£1.50

Question 13

F: In a sale all goods are reduced by 12%. How much will I save on a television which originally cost £200?

C: In a sale all goods are reduced by 12%. How much will I actually pay for a dress which originally cost £20?

A: In a sale all goods are reduced by 12%. If I actually pay £44 for a suit, how much did it originally cost?

Question 14

F: Look at the graph. At what time did the cyclist arrive at his destination?

C: Look at the graph. How long did the cyclist stop for on his journey?

A: Look at the graph. What was the average speed of the cyclist on his way home?

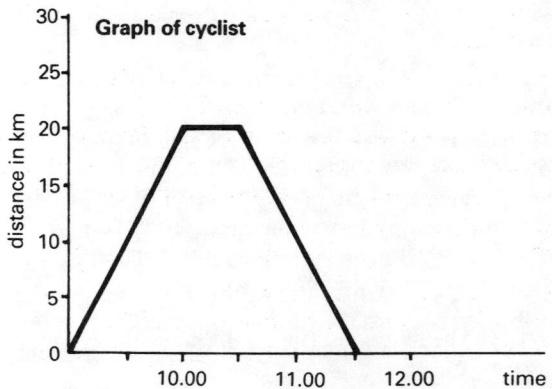

Question 15

F: Look at the graph. Which is the most popular group?

C: Look at the graph. How many people voted altogether?

A: Look at the graph. What was the mean number of votes scored by each group?

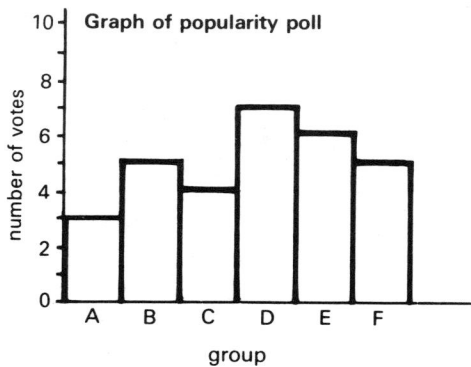

COURSEWORK

In the past, when assessing students' ability in mathematics, the main emphasis has been on testing a particular range of skills and techniques, the knowledge of certain facts, and the ability to solve problems of standard types. Within a timed examination, it has not been possible:

(a) to test practical skills;

(b) to enable students to do an extended piece of work;

(c) to collect, display and analyse real data in a statistics project;

(d) to allow students to show their problem-solving skills in unfamiliar situations.

All of these are desirable if you are going to be able to use your mathematical abilities in the real world in later life.

In mathematics, two broad 'domains' of abilities have been identified as an attempt to make sure that each of the above areas of work is given due attention. In general terms these two domains are:

Domain 1: Concepts, skills and procedures

Domain 2: Strategy, implementation and communication

The first domain covers such things as the use of appropriate symbols, the knowledge of facts, and the routine aspects of mental, oral, written and practical work, and includes the use of calculators and measuring and drawing instruments.

The second domain is more concerned with the ability to think mathematically, and with the use of strategies and processes in a variety of situations. It covers the ability:

(a) to formulate and interpret problems;
(b) to develop strategies for their solution;
(c) to identify and collect appropriate data;
(d) to evaluate and interpret results;
(e) to draw conclusions and communicate these by oral, written or graphical means.

Whilst, in the past, the items in the first domain, with the exception of the mental and oral aspects, have been tested by written examinations, and clearly many of the items in the second domain can only be tested by coursework, it is not intended that such an artificial split should be made. For example, you may find that the practical measuring aspects of the first domain are likely to be tested practically during coursework, whereas the ability to solve a geometrical problem, covered in the second domain, might well be tested in a timed examination.

Examples of coursework might include some or all of the following.

Practical geometry

This aspect could include:

(a) carrying out a simple survey of the school grounds;
(b) making scale drawings and perhaps a three-dimensional model;
(c) carrying out an investigation, or project, on wheels or gears.

Everyday applications of mathematics

This aspect could include:

(a) planning a cycling holiday on the continent;
(b) designing a new kitchen, including redecorating and retiling;
(c) carrying out an investigation into savings and interest rates.

Statistics and probability

This aspect could include:

(a) carrying out a survey of prices or products in local supermarkets;
(b) using sampling to gather information about a product or service;
(c) carrying out an investigation into probabilities with dice, etc.

Investigations and projects

This aspect could include:

(a) carrying out a number of small investigations or projects;
(b) carrying out one major investigation over a period of time;
(c) writing a study on a mathematical topic of an approved choice.

When coursework is being assessed, in addition to any results you may have obtained, attention will be given to the way you have collected the information for your project or investigation, the way you have set out this information and the various comments or conclusions you have drawn.

INVESTIGATIONS

In an investigation you are posed a problem or given a situation to explore. The solution to the problem will not be immediately obvious, and often you will have a free hand in deciding what direction to take.

You should realise that your approach to the situation, and commentary on what you are doing at each stage, are just as important as getting a well defined solution. In some cases there may not be a unique solution.

The example which follows is typical of a number of similar investigations. We shall look at the way it might be approached, and indicate the main stages that might be used in tackling an investigation of this type.

Investigate the number of tiles needed to put a border around a given shape

Stage 1: Getting some results
Let's start with a rectangle. For the first one (a), I need twelve tiles.

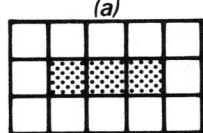
(a)

Let's try another one. For the second one (b), I need twenty-two tiles.

I don't seem to be getting very far, so let's try and be more systematic and draw up a table of results.

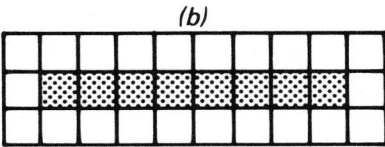
(b)

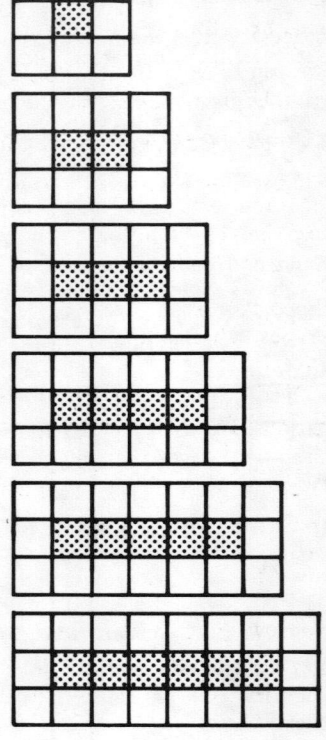

Stage 2: Being systematic

I will start at the beginning and complete the table.

Length	Number of tiles
1	8
2	10
3	12
4	14
5	16
6	?

There seems to be a pattern here. The numbers are going up in twos, so the next one should be 18. Does this work? Yes it does.

Stage 3: Finding a rule

Can I find a rule which will give me the number of tiles if I know the length of the rectangle? Can I describe the rule in words?

Ah ha! The number of tiles is six more than double the length. Can I describe this rule using symbols? $t = 2l + 6$

Stage 4: Testing and modifying the rule

Now let's try the rule with other rectangles. Oh dear! It doesn't seem to work.

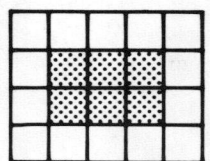

Recording is important. Let's look at how the border is made up. We need tiles for both lengths, both widths, and one for each corner. So the number of tiles is the length of the perimeter plus four tiles for the corners.

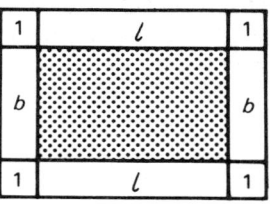

Stage 5: Justifying the result

We can draw a diagram for the general case. Using symbols, the rule is:

$$t = 2l + 2b + 4 \text{ or } t = 2(l + b) + 4$$

That seems to have cracked it.

Stage 6: Now what happens if . . . ?

Since this is an investigation, we ought to explore borders for other shapes. What about 'T' shapes, 'L' shapes or 'E' shapes?

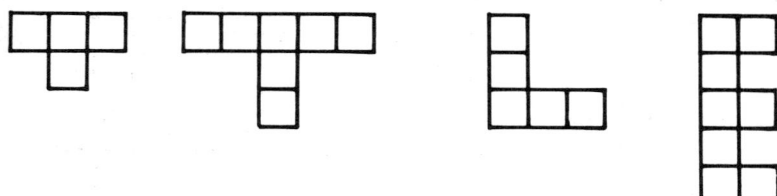

How much further you go will now depend on how much time you have been given for the investigation.

It is important to remember when doing a project or an investigation, that marks will be awarded for the presentation and recording of your results, and whether you have used some strategy or been systematic in your approach, and not just for the 'solution to the problem'.

SECTION 5

Specimen exam papers

In the last section we looked at school-based assessment, and now we consider the written exam papers. These will account for the largest part of the assessment, and before 1991 it may be possible for you to be assessed entirely by written papers. Even if you are being assessed partially by school-based work, the written exam will normally account for at least 50%, and possibly as much as 75%, of the assessment. So you will see that the written exam papers are of major importance.

Different exam groups use different systems for numbering their papers and offer different numbers of papers. In this section we have assumed the system of four papers which is used by most boards. Paper 1 is the easiest and Paper 4 the most difficult. Candidates take two papers. As was pointed out earlier in the book, you will be entered for the papers which are the most appropriate for your ability.

Either		**Paper 1** ⎱	target grade: F;
	and	**Paper 2** ⎰	grades available: E, F, G
Or		**Paper 2** ⎱	target grade: D;
	and	**Paper 3** ⎰	grades available: C, D, E, F
Or		**Paper 3** ⎱	target grade: B;
	and	**Paper 4** ⎰	grades available: A, B, C, D

The specimen exam papers which follow give examples of the kinds of questions you may expect to find in each paper. Different exam groups use a different style or length of paper, but questions will be based on topics selected from those in the lists given in section 3.

Papers 1 and 2 are based on topics in list 1 only. Paper 3 is based on topics in lists 1 and 2 only. Paper 4 is based on topics in all the lists. Each paper is marked out of 100, and the marks for each question are shown at the end of the question. Answers are given at the end of this section, and specimen solutions to some questions are set out and discussed in section 6.

PAPER 1

Time allowed 2 hours   Calculators may be used

Answer all questions

1 Copy and complete the following greengrocers' bill:

8 lb potatoes at 9p per lb;
3 lb carrots at 15p per lb;
2 cauliflowers at 35p each.

(4 marks)

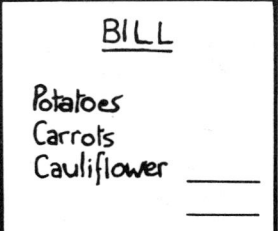

BILL

Potatoes
Carrots
Cauliflower ____

____

2 Alan, Brian, Carol and Deborah had a meal in a restaurant. Alan's meal cost £3.50, Brian's cost £4.25, Carol's cost £3.85 and Deborah's cost £3.20. Alan paid the bill for all the meals with a £20 note.

(a) How much change did he get?
(b) The four friends then decided to share the cost of the meals equally. How much did they each pay?

(5 marks)

3 A field in the shape of a rectangle is 250 m long and 180 m wide.

(a) Calculate its perimeter in metres.
(b) Calculate its area in square metres.
(c) Calculate its area in hectares, given that 1 hectare = 10 000m².

(4 marks)

4

	Distance from Coventry (miles)		
Coventry	0	dep. 09.40	dep. 19.30
Northampton	31	arr. 10.30	
		dep. 10.35	
Bedford	54	arr. 11.17	
		dep. 11.20	
Cambridge	85	arr. 12.15	

The time-table shows the times and distances of a bus journey from Coventry to Cambridge passing through Northampton and Bedford. Use the table to find:

(a) the distance from Northampton to Bedford;
(b) the time taken for the journey from Bedford to Cambridge;

(c) the time of arrival in Cambridge of the 19.30 bus from Coventry, given that the journey times are the same;

(d) the price of a return ticket from Coventry to Cambridge if the cost is calculated at a rate of 5p per mile.

(7 marks)

5 The formula for calculating the area of a right-angled triangle is $A = \frac{1}{2} bh$.

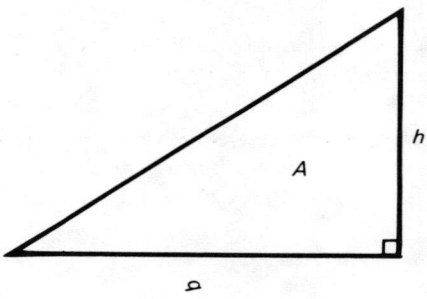

Calculate the area of each of the triangles below.

(4 marks)

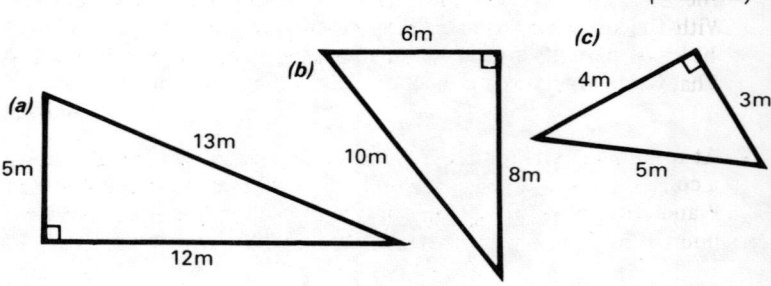

6 A 6 lb turkey costs £4.68.

(a) How much per lb is the turkey?

(b) For how long should it be cooked in a microwave oven, if the instruction book tells you to allow 13 minutes per lb?

(4 marks)

7

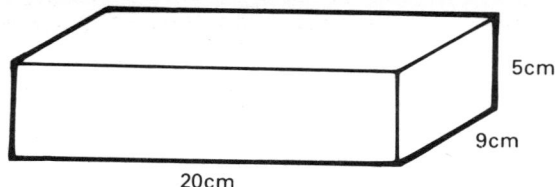

The diagram shows a brick in the shape of a cuboid with length 20 cm, breadth 9 cm and height 5 cm.
(a) How many faces does the brick have?
(b) How many edges does the brick have?
(c) Find the volume of the brick.

(4 marks)

8

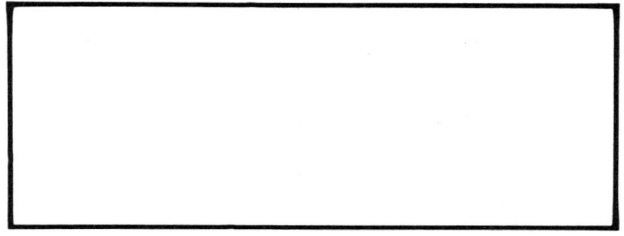

The diagram is a scale drawing of a rectangular plot of ground. With the scale used 1 cm represents 4 m. By measuring the sides of the drawing, find the actual measurements of the plot in metres. What is the area of the plot?

(5 marks)

9 At noon John sets out from a point P and walks in a straight line at a constant speed of 6 km per hour. At 1.00 p.m. Mary sets out from P and walks in a straight line in the opposite direction at 4 km per hour. How far apart are they at 2.00 p.m.?

(4 marks)

10 The owner of a car drove 12 000 miles in a year. The car averaged 30 miles to a gallon and throughout the year the cost of petrol was £1.80 per gallon. Other expenses involved in using the car were:

   Tax £100; Insurance £165; Servicing £95.

(a) Calculate the cost of petrol for the year.
(b) Calculate the total cost of running the car for the year.
(c) Calculate the average cost per mile of running the car for a year.

(7 marks)

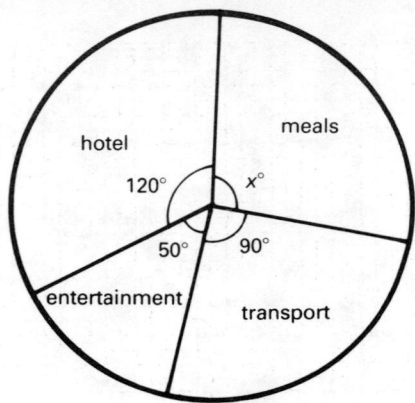

The pie chart represents the cost of a weekend in London. The hotel cost was £60.

(a) Calculate the angle marked $x°$.

(b) Calculate the cost of entertainment.

(c) Calculate the total cost of the weekend.

(d) Express the hotel cost as a fraction of the total cost of the weekend.

(7 marks)

12

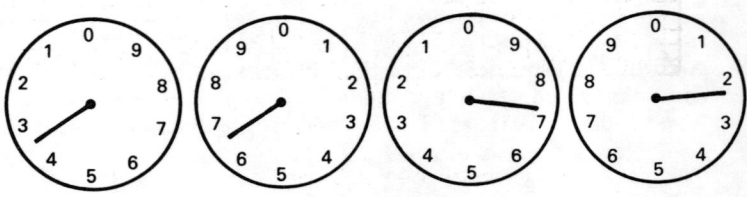

The dials above represent the reading on an electricity meter on a given date when the meter is read. Three months previously the meter reading had been 2427 units.

(a) State the reading shown by the dials above.

(b) How many units have been used in the past 3 months?

(c) The price per unit is 5.2 p and there is a standing charge of £6.50 per quarter. What will be the total amount owing for the past 3 months?

(8 marks)

13

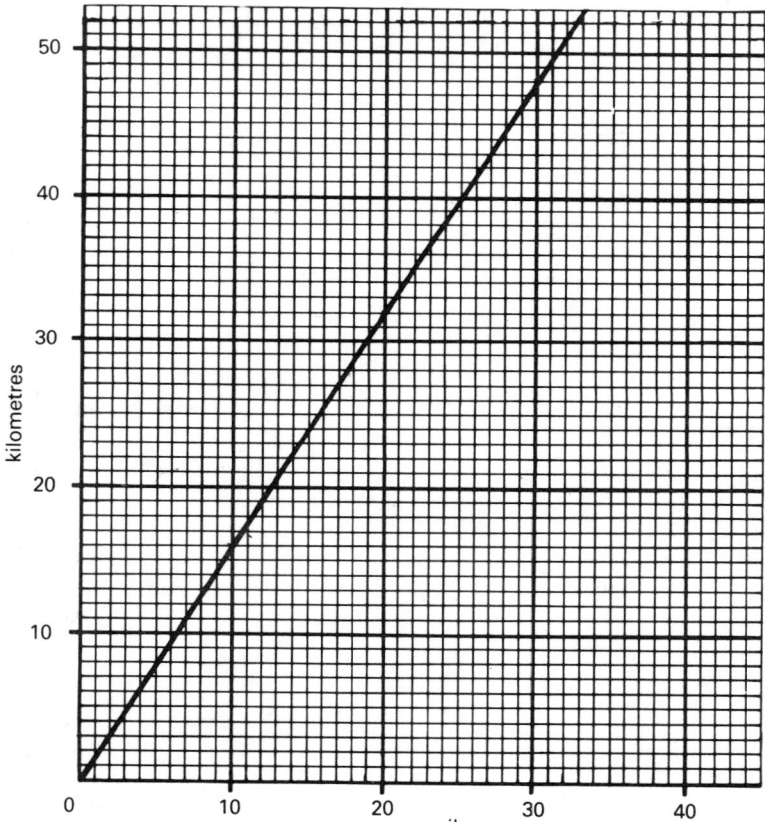

The graph converts miles to kilometres.

(a) Use the graph to convert:
  (i)   25 miles to kilometres;
  (ii) 28 kilometres to miles.

(b) Find the number of miles which are equal to 120 kilometres.

(7 marks)

14 A park has a circular flower-bed of radius 5 metres. Tulip bulbs are planted 20 cm apart all round the edge of the bed. Calculate the number of bulbs planted (take $\pi = 3.14$).

(4 marks)

15 In an experiment on word size, the number of letters in each word of a piece of writing was counted. The numbers were:

```
1  4  1  5  5  2  3  6  3  7
6  6  5  1  4  4  3  5  2  6
4  6  1  7  3  5  6  5  4  4
2  1  3  6  5  5  4  3  1  2
2  4  5  5  6  5  1  3  7  6
```

(a) How many words were counted?
(b) Copy and complete the frequency table.

Number of letters in a word	1	2	3	4	5	6	7
Frequency (number of words)							

(c) On graph paper, draw a bar chart to illustrate the above information.
(d) Which length of word was met most frequently?

(9 marks)

16 A van travels a distance of 174 kilometres along a motorway in 3 hours.

(a) Calculate its average speed in kilometres per hour.
(b) How far does it travel in 2½ hours if it maintains this speed?

(4 marks)

17 The drawing shows the pattern on the top half of a wall tile. The pattern on the tile is symmetrical about the line **AB**.

(a) Draw a picture of the whole tile.
(b) If the tile measures 10 cm by 10 cm, how many will be needed to cover a part of a wall measuring 2 m by 1.5 m?

(4 marks)

A television set at Ron's TV shop costs £350 including VAT. A similar set at Syd's shop costs £280 plus VAT. VAT is 15%.

(a) Calculate the total cost price, including VAT, at Syd's.

(b) Ron gives a discount of 5% off his total price, for cash. Calculate the price paid by a customer who pays cash at Ron's.

(c) Syd offers his set on hire-purchase. The terms are:

Deposit £60 plus 12 monthly payments of £24.

Calculate the total hire-purchase price of the set at Syd's.

(9 marks)

Answers are given on page 67.

PAPER 2

Time allowed 2 hours   Calculators may be used

Answer all questions

1   Use your calculator to find the value of $2\frac{3}{4}$ metres of material at £1.89 per metre. Give your answer to the nearest 1 p.

(4 marks)

2   A box holds 5.25 kg of oranges. Find how many oranges there are in the box if the average weight of an orange is 75 g.

(3 marks)

3   Washing-powder is sold in three sizes. The 3 kg size costs £2.75, the 2 kg size costs £1.74 and the 800 g size costs 88 p.

(a) What is the cost of 1 kg of powder if you buy the largest size? Give your answer to the nearest 1 p.

(b) What is the cost of 100 g of powder if you buy the smallest size?

(c) Which size is the best value for money? Show all your working.

(5 marks)

4   On a cold evening the temperature outside a house is −4°C. Inside the house the temperature is 12°C.

(a) How much higher is the temperature inside than outside?

(b) What will the outside temperature be if, during the night, it falls by 3°C?

(4 marks)

5   The ages of 5 children in a group are 13 years 1 month, 13 years 7 months, 12 years 6 months, 11 years 2 months and 13 years 5 months.

(a) Calculate the average (mean) age of the children.

(b) When a sixth child joins the group the average age becomes 12 years 10 months. What is the age of the sixth child?

(6 marks)

6   A bicycle wheel has a diameter of 70 cm.

(a) Calculate its circumference (use π = 3.14).

(b) Calculate how far the bicycle goes when the wheel turns through 20 complete revolutions.

(c) Through how many complete revolutions does the wheel turn when the bicycle travels 1 kilometre?

(7 marks)

7   John leaves home at the same time each day to walk to school. On most days, when he walks at his normal speed, the walk takes 20 minutes and he arrives at school 5 minutes early.

(a) How long does it take him on a day when he walks at twice his normal speed?

(b) How long does it take him on a day when he walks at only half his normal speed? By how many minutes is he late arriving at school?

(4 marks)

8   The graph represents the journey of a bus. The bus travelled from Birmingham to Oxford via Warwick, a distance of 64 miles. Use the graph to find:

(a) the time at which the bus arrived at Warwick;

(b) how long the bus stopped in Warwick;

(c) how far the bus was from Oxford at 10.30 a.m.

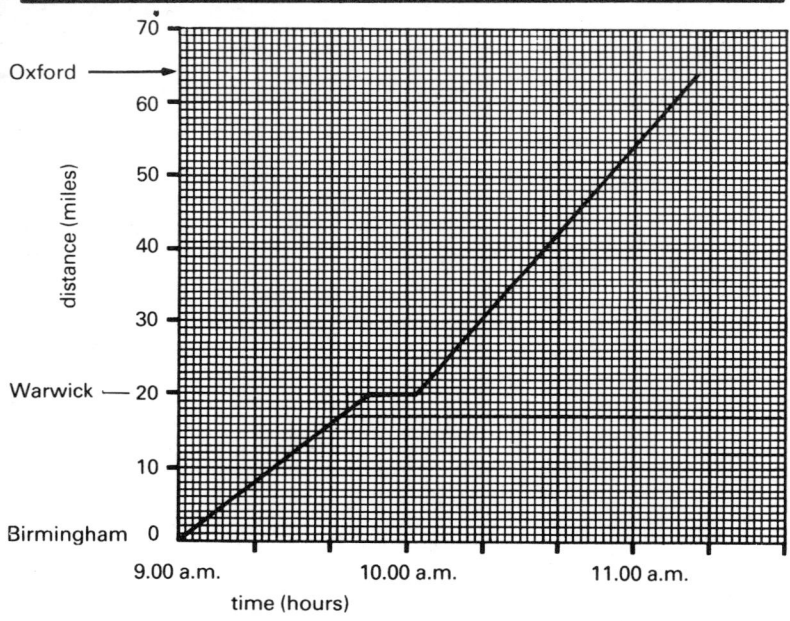

At 10.00 a.m. a car left Oxford and travelled at a constant speed to Warwick, arriving in Warwick at 11.15 a.m.

(d) On your graph paper, draw a line to represent the journey of the car.

(e) Use your graph to find the time at which the car met the bus.

(8 marks)

9 A supermarket employs extra staff at the weekend to help to stock the shelves. It employs 8 extra staff who each work from 9.30 a.m. until 1.30 p.m. without a break and are paid at the rate of £2.30 per hour. Calculate the total amount of money paid out by the supermarket to these extra staff.

(4 marks)

10 A ship sets out from a point A and sails in a straight line due north for 10 kilometres to a point B. It then turns and sails in a straight line in a direction north-west for 5 kilometres to a point C. It then turns again to sail directly back to A. On your paper make a scale drawing of the ship's journey, using a scale of 1 cm to represent 1 km. Measure the length AC on your drawing. Use this to find the total distance actually travelled by the ship on its journey.

(7 marks)

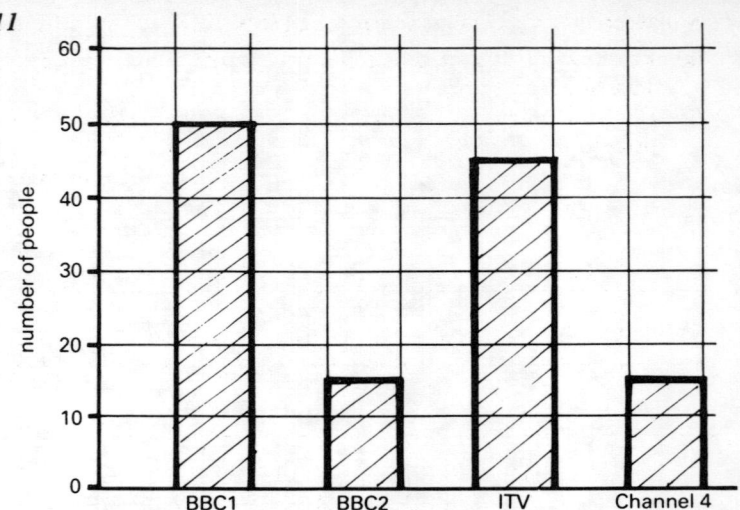

11 A survey was taken of the number of people in a district who were watching television at a given time one evening. The results are shown in the bar chart.

(a) How many people were watching television?
(b) How many more were watching ITV than Channel 4?
(c) What fraction of the total number of viewers in the survey was watching BBC 1? Express this as a decimal.

(5 marks)

12 Before going to the USA on holiday, a man changed £120 into dollars. One morning while on holiday he bought a book for $8.70. Given that the rate of exchange was $1.45 = £1, calculate:

(a) the number of dollars he received before going on holiday;
(b) the cost of the book in pounds.

(4 marks)

13 A bag contains 10 white, 6 red and 4 blue beads. A bead is drawn at random. Find the probability that it is:

(a) white;
(b) blue;
(c) not red.

If the first two beads removed are both white and they are not replaced, find the probability that the third bead selected will be:

(d) white;
(e) not white.

(7 marks)

14 A man bought a second-hand car for £1600.

(a) For how much should he sell it if he wants to make a profit of 10% of his cost price?

(b) For how much did he sell it if he made a loss of 5% of his cost price?

(4 marks)

15

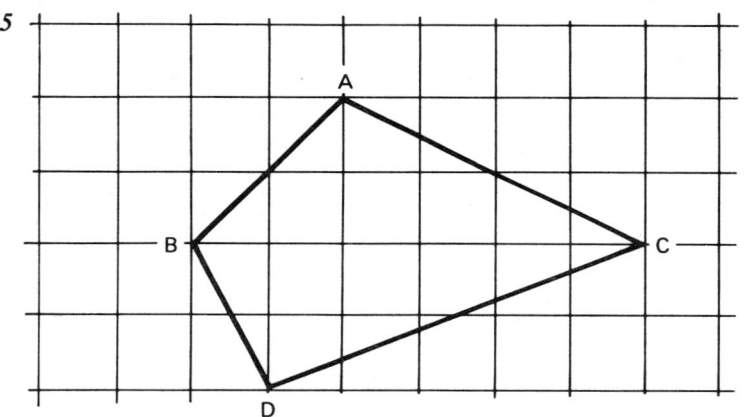

The shape ABDC is drawn on centimetre-squared paper.

(a) Write down the length BC.

(b) Calculate the area of triangle ABC.

(c) Calculate the area of the quadrilateral ABDC.

(d) Use your ruler to measure the length AC.

(e) Use your protractor to measure the size of angle BDC.

(9 marks)

16 A closed box is made of wood 3 cm thick. Its outside dimensions are:

    length 78 cm; width 56 cm; height 56 cm.

(a) What are its inside dimensions?

(b) Calculate the total surface area of the inside of the box.

(5 marks)

17 The shaded shape shown overleaf is the net of a solid. It is drawn on centimetre-squared paper.

(a) What is the name of the solid whose net this is?

(b) On your centimetre-squared paper, draw the same net as the one shown but with sides twice as long. Draw an axis of symmetry on your shape.

(c) If the net you have drawn was used to make a solid, what would be the volume of the solid?

(6 marks)

18 The children in a class measured their handspans. The results are shown in the table below.

Handspan (cm)	13	14	15	16	17	18
Number of children	2	3	9	7	6	2

(a) How many children were in the survey?
(b) Which length of handspan is the median?
(c) Which length is the mode?
(d) The children use their handspans to measure the width of a cupboard. A girl with a 15 cm handspan finds that the cupboard is 12 handspans wide. What would be the width of the cupboard in handspans if measured by the child with the largest handspan?

(8 marks)

Answers are given page 67.

PAPER 3

Time allowed 2 hours   Calculators may be used

Answer all questions

1 An engineer gives a measurement as 1.3×10^{-4}.
Write this as a decimal.

(2 marks)

2 The attendance at a football match is 46 570. Write this:

(a) to the nearest thousand;
(b) in standard form.

(3 marks)

3 Jane went shopping. In the first shop she spent one third of her money. In the second shop she spent half of the money remaining. She then had 40p. How much did she have originally?

(3 marks)

4 The formula to convert temperatures from degrees Celsius to degrees Fahrenheit is:

$$F = \frac{9}{5} C + 32$$

where F is the temperature in Fahrenheit and C is the temperature in Celsius.

(a) Find the temperature on the Fahrenheit scale which is the same as $30°C$.

(b) Find the temperature on the Celsius scale which is the same as $50°F$.

(c) Write an expression for C in terms of F.

(5 marks)

5 Three people share a sum of £4.20. How much do they each receive if:

(a) they share it equally;

(b) they share it in the proportion 2:2:3?

(4 marks)

6 On 1 January 1980 Susan invested £500 in a bank savings account. The interest paid by the bank is 8% on the sum of money in the account and this is added to the account on 31 December. On 1 January 1981 Susan invested another £500 in the same account. Calculate the amount in Susan's account on:

(a) 2 January 1981;

(b) 2 January 1982.

(4 marks)

7 The equation of a line PQ is $y + 3x = 5$ and the equation of line RS is $5x - 3y = 8$. Calculate:

(a) the gradient of PQ;

(b) the gradient of RS;

(c) the coordinates of the point where PQ cuts the y-axis;

(d) the coordinates of the point where RS cuts the x-axis.

(4 marks)

8 A train leaves a station A at 11.36 a.m. and travels 112 miles to a station B in $1\frac{3}{4}$ hours. Calculate:

(a) the arrival time at B;

(b) the average speed of the train for this journey;

(c) the price of a ticket for this journey, given that the price is calculated by charging 11.5p for each mile travelled.

(5 marks)

9 (a)

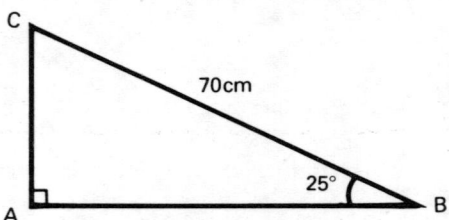

In the figure above, ABC is a triangle in which $B\hat{A}C = 90°$, $A\hat{B}C = 25°$ and BC = 70 cm. Calculate the length of AB, correct to one decimal place.

(b) A boat is 120 metres from the foot of a vertical cliff which is 45 metres high. Calculate the angle of elevation from the boat to the top of the cliff.

(c)

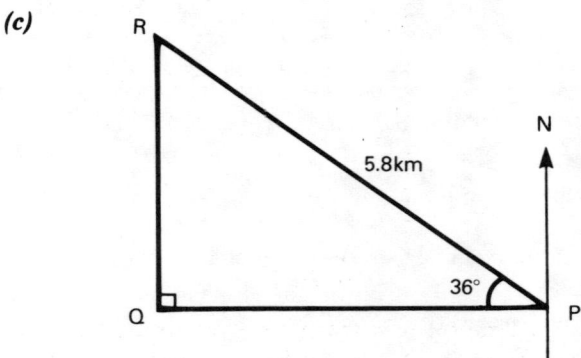

In the figure above, R is due north of Q, Q is due west of P, PR is 5.8 km and $R\hat{P}Q$ is 36°. Calculate:

(i)   the bearing of R from P;
(ii) the distance QR, correct to two decimal places.

(8 marks)

10

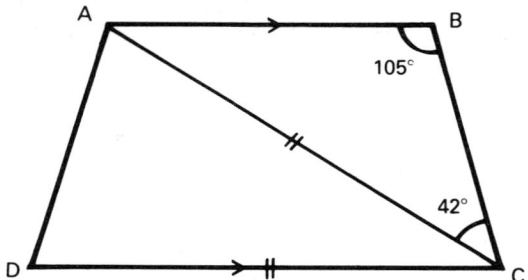

The diagram shows the cross section of a girder in which AB is parallel to DC, AC = DC, AB̂C = 105° and BĈA is 42°. Calculate:

(a) the size of angle ACD;
(b) the size of angle ADC.

(4 marks)

11

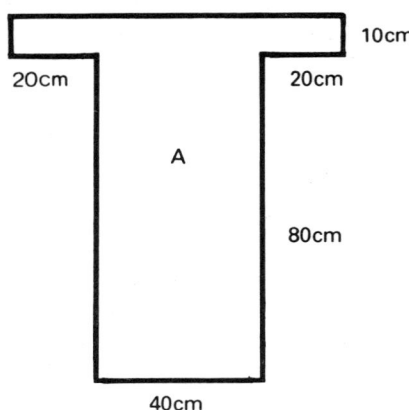

In the diagram above, A is the pattern for a simple smock. Two pieces of material such as A are needed to make the smock. A tailor has a piece of material which is in the shape of a rectangle 1 metre wide and 2 metres long and wants to use it to make two complete smocks (4 pieces).

On centimetre-squared paper, using a scale of 1 cm to represent 10 cm, draw a rectangle to represent the piece of material. On your rectangle, show how 4 pieces, each of shape A, could be cut from the material.

(a) What is the area of material unused?

(b) Express the unused area as a fraction of the total area of material.

(c) Express the unused area as a percentage of the total area of material.

(8 marks)

12 A lawn is in the shape of a rectangle 20 m long and 12 m wide. In the middle of the lawn there is a circular rose-bed of diameter 5 m.

(a) Calculate the area of the rose-bed (use $\pi = 3.14$).

(b) Fertiliser is to be put on the lawn at the rate of 25 g per square metre. Calculate the number of 1 kg packets of fertiliser required.

(7 marks)

13 AB is a diameter of a circle, centre O and radius 8 cm. The tangent to the circle at B passes through a point P. The length PB is 15 cm.

(a) Calculate the length OP.

(b) Calculate the length AP, giving your answer to 1 decimal place.

(4 marks)

14 The probability that Rovers will beat United at football is $\frac{3}{5}$. The probabability that United will win is $\frac{1}{4}$.

(a) What is the probability that there will be a draw?

(b) The two teams meet twice in a season. What is the probability that:

   (i) Rovers will win both games?

   (ii) Rovers will win the first and United will win the second game?

   (iii) Rovers will not win either game?

(8 marks)

15 A box contains coloured rods of different lengths. The number of rods of each length is given in the following table:

Length of rod	1 cm	2 cm	3 cm	4 cm	5 cm	6 cm
Number of rods	2	3	11	1	5	9

(a) What is the median length of rod?

(b) Calculate the mean length of rod.

(5 marks)

16 An engine part is made by drilling a cylindrical hole of diameter 3 cm through a solid cuboid of metal. The cuboid has length 8 cm, breadth 5 cm and height 4 cm and the axis of the cylindrical hole passes through the centres of the two largest faces. Calculate the volume of metal in the engine part (use $\pi = 3.14$).

(6 marks)

17 The commission charged by an estate agent when selling a house is 3% of the first £20 000 of the selling-price plus 2% of the remainder.

(a) Calculate the commission charged by the estate agent when a house is sold for £28 000.

(b) Find an expression in terms of x for the commission charged when a house is sold for £x, where x is greater than 20 000.

(c) Calculate the selling-price of a house on which the commission charged is £840.

(9 marks)

18 A manufacturer puts his product into packets whose base is a rectangle of area 36 cm².

He decides to experiment by trying different rectangular shapes, each with an area of 36 cm². In the table below, x is the length of the rectangle in centimetres and y is the breadth in centimetres.

x	1	2	3	4	6	12	18	36
y	36							
Area	36	36	36	36	36	36	36	36

(a) Copy and complete the table.

(b) Explain why the breadth of the rectangle can be given by the formula $y = \dfrac{36}{x}$.

(c) On your graph paper, draw the graph of the equation $y = \dfrac{36}{x}$, using values of x from 1 to 36.

(d) Use your graph to find:

    (i)   the breadth of the rectangle when the length is 5.5 cm;

    (ii) the perimeter of the rectangle when the breadth is 3.5 cm.

    (iii) the length and breadth of the rectangle when the perimeter is 26 cm.

(11 marks)

Answers are given on page 68.

PAPER 4

Time allowed $2\frac{1}{2}$ hours   Calculators may be used

Answer all questions

1 The length of a rectangle is twice its breadth. When a piece is cut off the rectangle by a line parallel to one of the shorter sides at a distance 3 cm from that side, the area of the remaining rectangle is 35 cm². Find the dimensions of the original rectangle.

(4 marks)

2 A man walks at a rate of p km per hour. Write an expression for the number of minutes he takes to walk x metres.

(3 marks)

3 A model of a building is made to a scale of 1:50. Calculate:
   (a) the actual length of a beam, in metres, if its length on the model is 8.4 cm;
   (b) the area of the cross section of the beam if its cross section area on the model is 0.28 cm^2;
   (c) the weight of the beam if its weight on the model is 1.15 g, and it is made of the same material.

(5 marks)

4 The formula $T = 2\pi \sqrt{\dfrac{l}{g}}$ gives the time of swing of a pendulum.
   (a) Calculate the value of T when $l = 80$, $g = 9.8$ and $\pi = 3.14$.
   (b) Rearrange the formula to give l in terms of T, π and g.

(5 marks)

5 A sum of money invested in a savings account increases by 10% each year.
   (a) If £1 is invested, how much will it be worth in one year's time? How much will it be worth in two years' time?
   (b) Write a formula to show how much £100 will be worth in n years' time.
   (c) Calculate the value of £100 after it has been invested for 8 years. Give your answer to the nearest 1 p.

(6 marks)

6 The fuel consumption of an engine varies directly as the square of the speed. If the engine uses 1 litre of fuel in travelling 10 km at a steady speed of 30 km per hour, how much fuel would it use in travelling 10 km at a steady speed of 40 km per hour?

(3 marks)

7 At the fruit stall in the market, a lady bought 6 oranges and 3 grapefruit for 75 p. Her friend bought 4 oranges and 5 grapefruit for 83 p.

Using x pence as the price of an orange and y pence as the price of a grapefruit, write down two equations in x and y.

Solve the equations.

What would be the cost of 5 oranges and 4 grapefruit?

(5 marks)

8

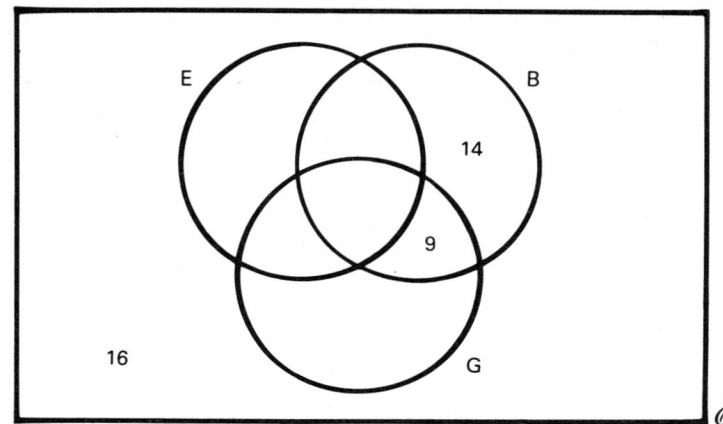

The 100 pupils in the fourth year at a comprehensive school can study biology **(B)**, economics **(E)** or geography **(G)**. Some of the numbers of pupils taking various combinations of these subjects are given in the Venn diagram above. In addition:

    5 pupils take all three subjects;
    22 take economics only;
    13 take economics and geography;
    41 take geography.

Copy and complete the Venn diagram, and below it write down the number of pupils who take:

(a) none of the subjects;
(b) biology and geography;
(c) economics and biology but not geography;
(d) geography only.

(6 marks)

9 A vertical tower stands on horizontal ground.

From a point P on the ground 30 m due south of the foot of the tower, the angle of elevation of the top of the tower is 58°. From the top of the tower the angle of depression of a point Q on the ground, due east of the tower, is 46°.

(a) Calculate the height of the tower.
(b) Calculate the distance from Q to the foot of the tower.
(c) Calculate the distance and bearing of Q from P.

(9 marks)

10 A is the point $(-2, 8)$, B is $(4, 0)$ and C is $(-3, 0)$. D is a point on the y-axis such that $CD = kAB$.

(a) Calculate the gradient of AB.
(b) Find the equation of the line CD.
(c) Write down the coordinates of D.
(d) Write down the value of k.
(e) What type of quadrilateral is ABDC?

(8 marks)

11 The functions f and g are defined by

$$f(x) = x^2 + 3x - 10, \qquad g(x) = 2x + 5.$$

Calculate:

(a) $f(-2)$;
(b) the values of x for which $f(x) = 0$;
(c) $f(g(1))$;
(d) $g(f(2))$.

(5 marks)

12 Solve the equation:

$$\frac{x}{4} - \frac{x+3}{5} = \frac{1}{2}$$

(3 marks)

13 A bag contains 4 white and 6 red beads. A bead is taken from the bag and not replaced. A second bead is then taken from the bag.
    Find the probability that:

(a) the first bead is white;
(b) the first bead is white and the second bead is red;
(c) both beads are red.

(5 marks)

14

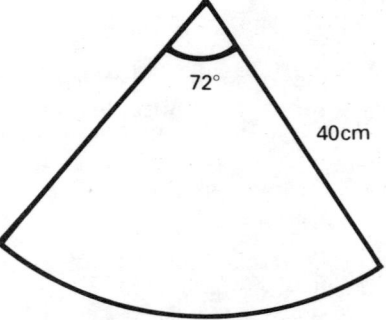

From a circular piece of paper of radius 40 cm, a sector of angle 72° is cut away. (See diagram above.) The sector has its straight edges joined, without overlap, to form a cone. Calculate:

(a) the area of the sector (use $\pi = 3.14$);

(b) the radius of the base of the cone;

(c) the height of the cone.

(9 marks)

15

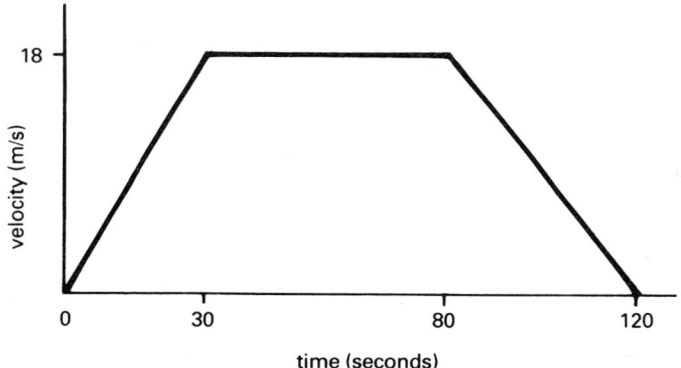

time (seconds)

In the graph, the velocity of a car is plotted against time. The car starts from rest and uniformly accelerates for 30 seconds. It then travels at a steady speed of 18 metres per second for 50 seconds. Finally it is uniformly brought to rest 2 minutes after it started. Calculate:

(a) the acceleration in the first 30 seconds;

(b) the total distance travelled in the 2 minutes.

(4 marks)

16 On squared paper, draw the triangle ABC, where A is (0, 2), B is (3, 0) and C is (3, 3).

$$\mathbf{P} = \begin{pmatrix} 1 & 0 \\ 0 & -1 \end{pmatrix} \text{ and } \mathbf{Q} = \begin{pmatrix} -1 & 0 \\ 0 & 1 \end{pmatrix}.$$

(a) Calculate **PQ**.

(b) On squared paper, draw the images of triangle ABC after the transformation determined by:

    (i) **P**;

    (ii) **Q**.

(c) Describe geometrically the transformations determined by:

    (i) **P**;

    (ii) **Q**;

    (iii) **PQ**.

17 Write down the two values missing from the following table, which gives values of $-x^2 + 5x - 3$ for values of x from 0 to 5.

x	0	0.5	1	1.5	2	2.5	3	3.5	4	4.5	5
$-x^2 + 5x - 3$	−3	−0.75	1	2.25	3		3	2.25		−0.75	−3

Draw the graph of $y = -x^2 + 5x - 3$ for values of x from 0 to 5. Use your graph to solve:

(a) $-x^2 + 5x - 3 = 0$;
(b) $x^2 - 5x + 1 = 0$.

(8 marks)

18

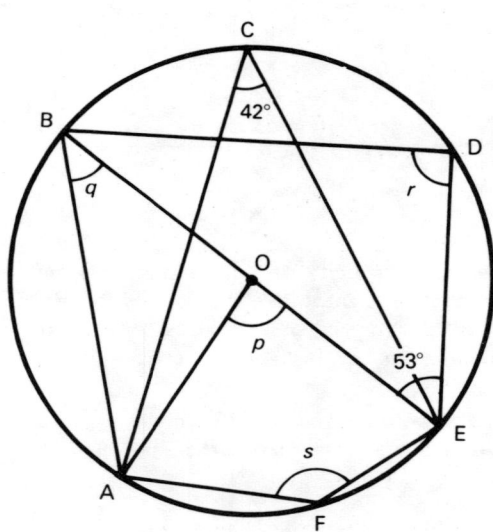

A, B, C, D, E and F are points on the circumference of a circle, centre O. BE is a diameter of the circle.

Given that $A\hat{C}E = 42°$, $B\hat{E}D = 53°$, write down the size of each of the angles p, q, r and s.

(4 marks)

Answers are given on page 68.

ANSWERS

Paper 1

1 £1.87
2 *(a)* £5.20   *(b)* £3.70
3 *(a)* 860 m   *(b)* 45 000 m²   *(c)* 4.5 ha
4 *(a)* 23 miles   *(b)* 55 minutes   *(c)* 22.05   *(d)* £8.50
5 *(a)* 30 m²   *(b)* 24 m²   *(c)* 6 m²
6 *(a)* 78 p   *(b)* 78 minutes
7 *(a)* 6   *(b)* 12   *(c)* 900 cm³
8 length 32 m   breadth 12 m   area 384 m²
9 16 km
10 *(a)* £720   *(b)* £1080   *(c)* 9 p
11 *(a)* 100°   *(b)* £25   *(c)* £180   *(d)* $\frac{1}{3}$
12 *(a)* 3672   *(b)* 1245   *(c)* £71.24
13 *(a)*(i) 40 km   (ii) 17.5 miles   *(b)* 75 miles
14 157
15 *(a)* 50   *(b)*

Number of letters	1	2	3	4	5	6	7
Frequency	7	5	7	8	11	9	3

(d) 5
16 *(a)* 58 km/hr   *(b)* 145 km
17 (b) 300
18 *(a)* £322   *(b)* £332.50   *(c)* £348

Paper 2

1 £5.20
2 70
3 *(a)* 92p   *(b)* 11 p   *(c)* 2 kg size
4 *(a)* 16°   *(b)* −7°
5 *(a)* 12 years 9 months   *(b)* 13 years 3 months
6 *(a)* 219.8 cm   *(b)* 43.96 m   *(c)* 454
7 *(a)* 10 minutes   *(b)* 40 minutes   *(c)* 15 minutes late
8 *(a)* 9.50 a.m.   *(b)* 12 minutes   *(c)* 28 miles   *(d)* 10.39 a.m.
9 £73.60
10 AC = 14 cm;   total distance is 29 km
11 *(a)* 125   *(b)* 30   *(c)* $\frac{2}{5}$, 0.4
12 *(a)* $174   *(b)* £6
13 *(a)* $\frac{1}{2}$ *(b)* $\frac{1}{5}$ *(c)* $\frac{7}{10}$ *(d)* $\frac{4}{9}$ *(e)* $\frac{5}{9}$
14 *(a)* £1760   *(b)* £1520
15 *(a)* 6 cm   *(b)* 6 cm²   *(c)* 12 cm²   *(d)* 4.5 cm   *(e)* 95°
16 *(a)* length 72 cm; width 50 cm; height 50 cm   *(b)* 19 400 cm²
17 *(a)* cube   *(c)* 8 cm³
18 *(a)* 29   *(b)* 16 cm   *(c)* 15 cm   *(d)* 10 handspans

Paper 3

1 0.000 13
2 *(a)* 47 000 *(b)* 4.657×10^4
3 £1.20
4 *(a)* 86°F *(b)* 10°C *(c)* $\dfrac{5(F-32)}{9}$
5 *(a)* £1.40 *(b)* £1.20; £1.20; £1.80
6 *(a)* £1040 *(b)* £1123.20
7 *(a)* -3 *(b)* $\frac{5}{3}$ *(c)* $(0, 5)$ *(d)* $(\frac{8}{5}, 0)$
8 *(a)* 1.21 p.m. *(b)* 64 m.p.h. *(c)* £12.88
9 *(a)* 63.4 cm *(b)* 20.56° *(c)*(i) 306° (ii) 3.41 km
10 *(a)* 33° *(b)* 73.5°
11 *(a)* 4000 cm² *(b)* $\frac{1}{5}$ *(c)* 20%
12 *(a)* 19.625 m² *(b)* 6 packets
13 *(a)* 17 cm (ii) 21.9 cm
14 *(a)* $\frac{3}{20}$ *(b)* (i) $\frac{9}{25}$ (ii) $\frac{3}{20}$ (iii) $\frac{4}{25}$
15 *(a)* 3 cm *(b)* 4 cm
16 131.74 cm³
17 *(a)* £760 *(b)* $\frac{1}{50} x + 200$ *(c)* £32 000
18 *(d)* (i) 6.5 cm (ii) 27 cm (iii) 9 cm, 4 cm

Paper 4

1 5 cm, 10 cm
2 $\dfrac{6x}{100p}$
3 *(a)* 4.2 m *(b)* 700 cm² *(c)* 143.75 kg
4 *(a)* 17.94 *(b)* $\dfrac{T^2 g}{4\pi^2}$
5 *(a)* £1.10, £1.21 *(b)* $100 \times (1.1)^n$ *(c)* £214.36
6 $1\frac{7}{9}$ litres
7 $x = 7$, $y = 11$; 79 p
8 *(a)* 16 *(b)* 14 *(c)* 7 *(d)* 19
9 *(a)* 48.01 m *(b)* 46.36 m *(c)* 55.22 m, 57.09°
10 *(a)* $-\frac{4}{3}$ *(b)* $3y + 4x + 12 = 0$ *(c)* $(0, -4)$ *(d)* $\frac{1}{2}$ *(e)* trapezium
11 *(a)* -12 *(b)* $-5, 2$ *(c)* 60 *(d)* 5
12 $x = 22$
13 *(a)* $\frac{2}{5}$ *(b)* $\frac{4}{15}$ *(c)* $\frac{1}{3}$
14 *(a)* 1004.8 cm² *(b)* 8 cm *(c)* 39.2 cm
15 *(a)* 0.6 m s⁻² *(b)* 1530 m

16 *(a)* $\begin{pmatrix} -1 & 0 \\ 0 & -1 \end{pmatrix}$

   (c) (i) reflection in *x*-axis
       (ii) reflection in *y*-axis
       (iii) rotation, 180°, about origin

17 Missing values are 3.25 and 1
   (a) 4.3, 0.7   *(b)* 4.8, 0.2

18 $p = 84°$; $q = 42°$; $r = 90°$; $s = 138°$

SECTION 6

What are the examiners looking for?

This section looks at the way in which marks on the written exam papers are allocated. By considering different solutions, some correct and some incorrect, and by looking at the marks which would be given in each case, it aims to help you to avoid losing marks unnecessarily. The questions considered are all taken from the specimen exam papers in section 5.

Frequently candidates in a mathematics examination lose marks for reasons which are non-mathematical. These include errors such as:

misreading the question;
not giving all the working;
crossing out correct work;
approximating too early;
not giving answers to the correct degree of accuracy;
giving incorrect or no units.

Each of these common errors is discussed and indications are given of the steps which should be taken to avoid them.

WHICH METHOD?

Maths exams are different from exams in most other subjects, in that the questions often lead to a single correct answer. In general this means that if you obtain this correct answer by a correct method then you will get full marks. The method you use does not usually matter.

There are exceptions to this general rule. Sometimes a particular method is specified and it is then important to use that method. Consider Paper 1, question 5, for example. In this question you are given a number of triangles and are asked to: 'Calculate the area of each of the triangles.' The important word here is 'calculate'. If you attempt to do this question by drawing the triangles to scale on squared paper and then finding the areas by counting squares, you will not be given the marks.

70

A similar remark can be made about many questions involving trigonometry. In Paper 3, question 9(a) (p. 58), you are given a triangle and asked to: 'Calculate the length of AB.' You will not gain any marks if you draw the triangle to scale and then find the length of AB by measuring.

The important point to remember in both the above examples is that the word 'calculate' means that you are intended to perform a calculation and not do a scale drawing. The examiners will probably be testing your ability to draw to scale elsewhere in the paper.

Another example of a question which asks for a particular method is Paper 4, question 17. In this question, you are asked to draw the graph of $y = -x^2 + 5x - 3$, and then to: 'Use your graph to solve the equation $-x^2 + 5x - 3 = 0$.' The key words here are: 'Use your graph'. If you decide to solve the equation by some other method, then you will be wasting valuable exam time, as you will not gain marks, even though you may solve the equation correctly and probably do more work by using a non-graphical method. The point here is that the question was intended to test whether or not you could read a graph, and not your ability to solve equations.

The above examples demonstrate that certain questions specify a particular method and it is then important that you should carry out the instructions given. However, the majority of questions do not indicate any specific method and the normal rule which examiners then adopt is: *A correct answer by a correct method will gain full marks, irrespective of the method used*.

But what if your answer is wrong? Does this mean that you get no marks? No, of course not. To see just how many marks you might gain, you need to understand the types of marks which are given.

HOW MARKS ARE ALLOCATED

Types of marks

We have said already that correct answers by sound methods will gain full marks. Consequently when devising a mark scheme in maths, examiners need to give most consideration to the way in which marks should be allocated when a candidate does not obtain the correct answer. In order to do this two types of marks are awarded. *Method marks* are awarded when a candidate has the correct intention to carry out the necessary operation. *Accuracy marks* are awarded when the operation has been performed correctly. We shall refer to these as *M* marks and *A* marks.

Note that method marks are given for having the correct *intention*, not for performing the operation correctly. However, as we shall discuss later, an examiner can only judge your intention from what you have written on paper and not from your thoughts. Note also that accuracy marks are not simply awarded for the final answer: they may be given for correctly performing part of a solution.

In the next few pages, we consider the ways in which both kinds of marks are awarded, by looking at solutions, both correct and incorrect, to some of the questions in the specimen papers. The mark schemes suggested are an *indication* of how answers are assessed and are *not intended to be definitive*. The mark schemes used in the actual examination will have been agreed upon by a panel of examiners and will be used by all the examiners.

PAPER 1, QUESTION 2 *See page 45.*

Correct solution

(a) 3.50
       4.25   20.00
       3.85   −14.80
       3.20   5.20
      14.80

Answer: He received £5.20 change.

(b) 14.80 ÷ 4 = 3.70

Answer: They each paid £3.70.

This correct solution would receive full marks.

Mark scheme (5 marks in total)
(a) (*2 marks*) One method mark (*M1*) for adding the four amounts and subtracting from £20. One accuracy mark (*A1*) for obtaining the correct answer of £5.20.
(b) (*3 marks*) One method mark (*M1*) for adding the four amounts and dividing by 4. Two accuracy marks (*A2*) for the correct answer of £3.70.

Incorrect solution

(a) 3.50
       4.25   20.00
       3.85   −14.80
       3.20   6.20*
      14.80

Answer: He received £6.20 change.

(b) $14.80 \div 4 = 3.60*$

Answer: They each paid £3.60.

Both of these answers are incorrect. The errors are indicated by asterisks. However in part *(a)*, the candidate did have the correct intention. The working shows that the four amounts were added up and subtracted from £20, even if the subtraction was incorrect. The one method mark should be awarded. Also in part *(b)* the candidate clearly intended to divide £14.80 by 4. The answer was wrong but the method was the correct one. The one method mark should again be awarded. Consequently this solution gains 2 of the 5 marks.

PAPER 1, QUESTION 11 *See page 48.*

Correct solution

(a) $120 + 50 + 90 = 260$
  $360 - 260 \quad = 100$

  Answer: $100°$

(b) $120°$ represents £60
  $2°$ represents £1
  $50°$ represents £25

  Answer: £25

(c) $120°$ represents £60
  $360°$ represents £180

  Answer: £180

(d) Hotel cost is $\frac{120}{360}$ of total cost.

  Answer: $\frac{1}{3}$

This correct solution would receive full marks.

Mark scheme (7 marks in total)
(a) *(2 marks) M1* for adding 120, 50 and 90 and then subtracting from 360. *A1* for the correct answer of $100°$.
(b) *(2 marks) M1* for realising that $2°$ represents £1. *A1* for correct answer of £25.
(c) *(2 marks) M1* for multiplying 60 by 3 (or dividing 360 by 2). *A1* for correct answer of £180.
(d) *(1 mark) A1* for correct answer of $\frac{1}{3}$.

Incorrect solution

(a) $120 + 50 + 90 = 250*$
  $360 - 250 \quad = 110$

  Answer: $110°$

(b) 120° represents £60
    1° represents £2*
   50° represents £100

Answer: £100

(c) 120° represents £60
  360° represents £180

Answer: £180

(d) Answer: $\frac{1}{5}$*

In part *(a)* the three angles have been added together and the sum has then been subtracted from 360°. The addition was wrong but the intention was correct. *M1* will be given. In part *(b)* no marks will be given as the method is clearly wrong. Part *(c)* is correct and is given both marks. Part *(d)* is incorrect and since there are no marks for method in this part, no marks can be given. This incorrect solution gains 3 marks.

PAPER 2, QUESTION 6   *See page 52.*

Correct solution

(a) $C = \pi d$
  $C = 3.14 \times 70$
  $C = 219.8$

Answer: Circumference is 219.8 cm.

(b) In 1 revolution bicycle goes 219.8 cm.
  In 20 revolutions bicycle goes (219.8×20) cm = 4396 cm.

Answer: Bicycle travels 43.96 m.

(c) 1 km = 1000 m = 100 000 cm
  Number of revolutions is $100\,000 \div 219.8 = 454.959\ldots$

Answer: Number of complete revolutions is 454.

This correct solution would receive full marks.

Mark scheme (7 marks in total)
(a) (*2 marks*) *M1* for correctly substituting into the correct formula $C = \pi d$. *A1* for correct answer $C = 219.8$ cm.
(b) (*2 marks*) *M1* for multiplying the circumference by 20. *A1* for correct answer of 43.96 m.
(c) (*3 marks*) *M1* for dividing 1 km by the circumference. *A1* for 454.9 ... and a further *A1* for 454.

Incorrect solution

(a) $C = \pi d$
   $C = 3.14 \times 70$
   $C = 219.8$

   Answer: Circumference is 219.8 cm

(b) In 20 revolutions bicycle goes (219.8 × 20) cm = 4286 cm*

   Answer: Bicycle travels 42.86 m.

(c) Number of revolutions is 100 000 ÷ 219.8 = 454.959 . . .

   Answer: Number of revolutions is 455.*

Here the solution to part *(a)* is correct and would get 2 marks. In part *(b)*, the method is correct, but there is an error in the multiplication. The *M* mark will be awarded. In part *(c)*, the method is correct and so is the division, but the answer has been given correct to the nearest whole number. This would be given the *M1* and the first *A1* but not the final *A1*. This incorrect solution would get 5 of the 7 marks available.

PAPER 2, QUESTION 12 *See page 54.*

Correct solution

(a) Number of dollars is 120 × 1.45 = 174
   Answer: $174

(b) Cost of book is £8.70 ÷ 1.45 = £6
   Answer: £6

This correct solution would receive full marks.

Mark scheme (4 marks in total)

(a) (*2 marks*) *M1* for multiplying 120 by 1.45. *A1* for the correct answer of $174.

(b) (*2 marks*) *M1* for dividing 8.70 by 1.45. *A1* for correct answer of £6.

Incorrect solution

(a) Number of dollars is 120 × 1.45 = 17 400*
   Answer: $17 400

(b) Cost of book is £8.70 ÷ 1.45 = £60*

   Answer: £60

In both parts of this solution the method is correct but the answers are incorrect. The *M* marks would be awarded in both parts. This incorrect solution would receive 2 of the 4 marks.

Clearly it is not possible to give examples of all types of error but the incorrect solutions above should have given you an appreciation of how marks are allocated when some kinds of mistakes are made. The next few examples are chosen to illustrate a variety of mathematical situations. They include mark schemes and correct solutions.

PAPER 3, QUESTION 12 *See page 60.*

Solution

(a) Area of circle is πr^2
Area is $(3.14 \times 2.5 \times 2.5)\,\text{m}^2 = 19.625\,\text{m}^2$
Answer: Area of rose-bed is $19.625\,\text{m}^2$.

(b) Total area is $(20 \times 12)\,\text{m} = 240\,\text{m}^2$
Area of lawn is $(240 - 19.625)\,\text{m}^2 = 220.375\,\text{m}^2$
Number of grams of fertiliser is 220.375×25
Number of packets of fertiliser is $200.375 \times 25 \div 1000 = 5.509\ldots$
Answer: 6 packets are required.

Mark scheme (7 marks in total)
(a) (*2 marks*) *M1* for correctly substituting into $A = \pi r^2$. *A1* for correct answer of $19.625\,\text{m}^2$.
(b) (*5 marks*) *M1* for multiplying 20 by 12 to find total area. *M1* for subtracting the area of the circle from this total area. *M1* for multiplying this resultant area by 25. *A1* for obtaining $5.509\ldots$ and a further *A1* for correct answer of 6 packets.

PAPER 3, QUESTION 13 *See page 60.*

Solution

(a) From Pythagoras',
$\text{OP}^2 = \text{OB}^2 + \text{BP}^2$
$\text{OP}^2 = 8^2 + 15^2 = 64 + 225$
$\text{OP}^2 = 289$
$\text{OP} = 17$
Answer: OP is 17 cm

(b) $\text{AP}^2 = \text{AB}^2 + \text{BP}^2$
$\text{AP}^2 = 16^2 + 15^2 = 256 + 225$
$\quad\quad\; = 481$
$\text{AP} = \sqrt{481} = 21.93\ldots$
Answer: AP is 21.9 cm correct t
1 decimal place.

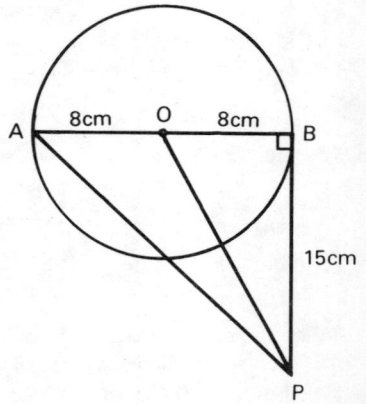

PAPER 4, QUESTION 9 *See page 63.*

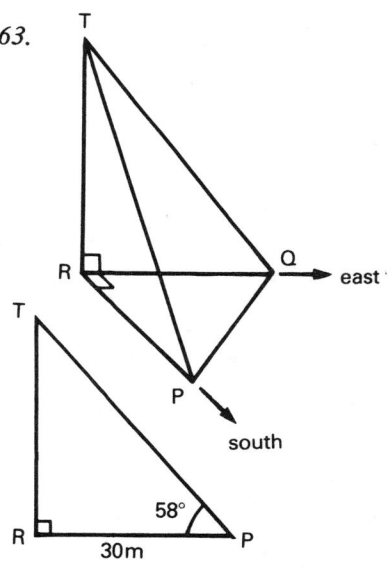

Solution

(a) Let the foot of the tower be **R** and the top of the tower be **T**.

$$\tan R\hat{P}T = \frac{TR}{RP}$$

$$\tan 58° = \frac{TR}{30}$$

$TR = 30 \times \tan 58° = 48.010 \ldots$

Answer: Height of tower is 48.01 m.

(b) $T\hat{Q}R = 46°$. So $Q\hat{T}R = 44°$.

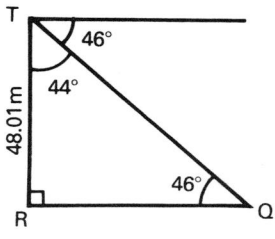

$$\tan Q\hat{T}R = \frac{QR}{TR} \quad \tan 44° = \frac{QR}{48.01}$$

$QR = 48.01 \times \tan 44° = 46.36 \ldots$

Answer: Distance from Q to foot of tower is 46.36 m.

(c) $QP^2 = QR^2 + RP^2$

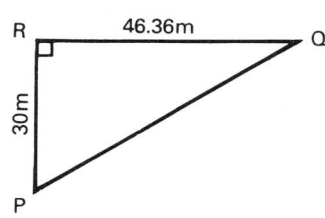

$\quad\quad = 46.36^2 + 30^2$

$\quad\quad = 2149 + 900 = 3049$

$QP = 55.217 \ldots$

$$\tan R\hat{P}Q = \frac{RQ}{RP} = \frac{46.36}{30} = 1.545$$

$R\hat{P}Q = 57.09°$

Answer: Q is 55.22 m from P on a bearing 57.09°.

(a) *(2 marks) M1* for correct use of the ratio $\tan R\hat{P}T = \dfrac{TR}{RP}$. *A1* for correct answer of 48.01 m.

(b) *(3 marks) M1* for knowing which is the angle of depression. *M1* for a correct trigonometric ratio, either $\tan Q\hat{T}R = \dfrac{QR}{TR}$ or $\tan T\hat{Q}R = \dfrac{TR}{QR}$. *A1* for correct answer of 46.36 m.

(c) *(4 marks) M1* for correct use of Pythagoras'. *A1* for correct answer of 55.22 m. *M1* for use of the ratio $\tan R\hat{P}Q = \dfrac{RQ}{RP}$. *A1* for correct bearing of 57.09°.

PAPER 4, QUESTION 14 *See page 64.*

Solution

(a) Area of sector is $\frac{72}{360}$ of the area of the circle.

$$\begin{aligned}
\text{Area of sector} &= \tfrac{72}{360} \times \pi r^2 \\
&= \tfrac{1}{5} \times 3.14 \times 40 \times 40 \\
&= 1004.8
\end{aligned}$$

Answer: Area of sector = 1004.8 cm.

(b) Length of arc is $\frac{72}{360} \times \pi d$

$$\begin{aligned}
&= \tfrac{1}{5} \times 3.14 \times 80 \\
&= 50.24
\end{aligned}$$

So circumference of circular base is 50.24 cm.
$2\pi R = 50.24$ where R is radius of base.
$R = \dfrac{50.24}{6.28}$ so $R = 8$

Answer: Radius of base is 8 cm.

(c) Let height of cone be H.

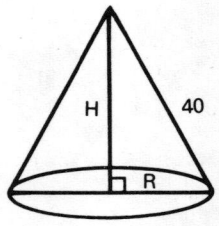

$$\begin{aligned}
H^2 + R^2 &= 40^2 \\
H^2 + 8^2 &= 40^2 \\
H^2 &= 1600 - 64 = 1536 \\
H &= 39.19
\end{aligned}$$

Answer: Height of cone is 39.2 cm (correct to 3 significant figures).

Mark scheme (9 marks in total)
(a) *(3 marks) M1* for knowing area of sector is $\frac{72}{360}$ of area of circle.

M1 for correct substitution into $\frac{72}{360} \times \pi r^2$. *A1* for correct answer of 1004.8 cm.

(b) (*4 marks*) *M1* for knowing length of arc is $\frac{1}{5}$ of circumference. *M1* for putting this arc length equal to circumference of base.
(Alternatively *M2* for putting circumference of base equal to $\frac{1}{5}$ of circumference of circular piece of paper.) Then *A2* for correct answer of 8 cm.

(c) (*2 marks*) *M1* for correct use of Pythagoras'. *A1* for correct answer of 39.19 or 39.2 cm.

The 'follow through' procedure

In some questions, an answer to one part of the question is used in later parts of the question. Consequently, an arithmetic error made early in the solution might mean that all subsequent working is incorrect. The result, unless steps are taken to remedy it, is that more marks will be lost from an error made early in the solution than from a similar error made later.

The remedy is for examiners to use what is known as the 'follow through' procedure. Provided the method of solution is correct, working after a previous error is followed through and, if no further error is made, the accuracy mark is given. This is illustrated in the next two examples.

PAPER 1, QUESTION 10 *See page 47.*

Correct solution

(a) Number of gallons used was 12 000 ÷ 30 = 400
Cost of petrol was £1.80 x 400 = £720

Answer: Cost of petrol was £720.

	£
(b) Petrol	720
Tax	100
Insurance	165
Servicing	95
Total	1080

Answer: Total cost of running car was £1080.

(c) Cost per mile was £1080 ÷ 12 000 = £0.09 = 9 p

Answer: Average cost per mile was 9 p.

This correct solution would receive full marks.

Mark scheme (7 marks in total)

(a) *(3 marks)* *M1* for dividing 12 000 by 30. *M1* for multiplying by 1.80. *A1* for correct answer of £720.

(b) *(2 marks)* *M1* for adding the four amounts. *A1* for the correct answer of £1080.

(c) *(2 marks)* *M1* for dividing £1080 by 12 000. *A1* for the correct answer of £0.09 or 9 p.

Incorrect solution

(a) Number of gallons used was 12 000 ÷ 30 = 400
Cost of petrol was £1.80 × 400 = £72*

Answer: Cost of petrol was £72.

(b)
	£
Petrol	72
Tax	100
Insurance	165
Servicing	95
Total	432

Answer: Total cost of running car was £432.

(c) Cost per mile was £432 ÷ 12 000 = £0.036 = 3.6 p

Answer: Average cost per mile was 3.6 p.

In this solution the methods throughout are correct and all the method marks are gained, but all three answers are wrong. However, the only mistake made is in part (a), when multiplying 1.80 by 400, and this does not deserve to lose the accuracy marks for all three parts of the question. In the second and third parts of the solution the working will be followed through and, since no further errors have been made the accuracy marks for those parts will be given. As a result, despite the error, the incorrect solution may gain 6 of the 7 possible marks.

PAPER 3, QUESTION 11 *See page 59.*

Correct solution

(a) There are 40 squares (1 cm by 1 cm) on the squared paper unused. Each square represents an area of 100 cm² of material.
Hence area of material unused is 4000 cm²

Answer: Area of unused material is 4000 cm².

(b) Total number of squares (1 cm by 1 cm) on the squared paper, representing the piece of material, is 10 × 20 = 200 squares.
So fraction of material is $\frac{40}{200} = \frac{1}{5}$.

Answer: $\frac{1}{5}$ of the material is unused.

80

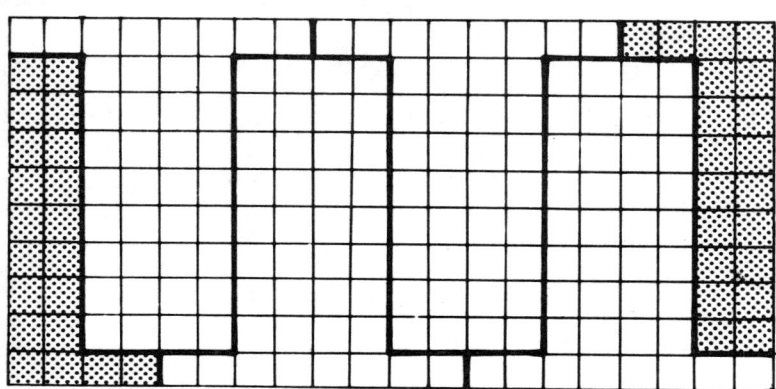

(c) $\frac{1}{5}$ = 20%.

Answer: 20% of the material is unused.

This correct solution would receive full marks.

Incorrect solution

(a) There are 20 squares* (1 cm by 1 cm) on the squared paper unused. Each square represents an area of 100 cm² of material. Hence area of unused material is 2000 cm².

Answer: Area of unused material is 2000 cm².

(b) Total number of squares (1 cm by 1 cm) on the squared paper, representing the piece of material, is 10 × 18 = 180 squares.* So fraction of material is $\frac{20}{180} = \frac{1}{9}$ *.

Answer: $\frac{1}{9}$ of the material is unused.

(c) $\frac{1}{9}$ = 11%.

Answer: 11% of the material is unused.

There is an error in part (a), but a further error in part (b) means that no accuracy marks can be given, even after following through the working.

COMMON ERRORS

The reasons for making errors in mathematics exam are many and varied. Some may be caused by lack of adequate preparation before the day. But there are a number of errors which are commonly made and which, with a little bit of thought, might be avoided. Some of these are now described.

Misreading the question

This is a very frequent cause of error. If a question is not read carefully then, in the rush of a timed exam, it is easy for it to be misread or misinterpreted. Sometimes it is a simple case of the misreading of a number; 3.84 is written instead of 3.48, say. At other times it may be that, because the question looks familiar, you don't bother to read it carefully, and then answer a question which is quite different from the one asked.

In the latter case, the result may be a loss of all marks available in the question. Even in the case of the simple misreading of a number you may be letting yourself in for a lot of extra work as the resulting calculation may be much more difficult than the one intended. The following two examples illustrate this.

PAPER 1, QUESTION 1 *See page 45.*

Correct solution

	p
8 lb potatoes at 9 p per lb	72
3 lb carrots at 15 p per lb	45
2 cauliflower at 35 p each	70
	187

Answer: Total bill is £1.87.

This bill is correctly completed and would gain full marks.

Incorrect solution

	p
8 lb potatoes at 9 p per lb	72
3 lb carrots at 16 p per lb	48*
2 cauliflower at 35 p each	70
	190

Answer: Total bill is £1.90.

This bill is incorrect, as the price of carrots has been misread as 16 p. This has not led to any extra work, but some marks will be lost.

PAPER 4, QUESTION 7 *See page 62.*

Correct solution

First equation	$6x + 3y$	$= 75$	(i)
Second equation	$4x + 5y$	$= 83$	(ii)

Multiply equation (i) by 5 and equation (ii) by 3.

$$30x + 15y = 375 \quad \text{(iii)}$$
$$12x + 15y = 249 \quad \text{(iv)}$$

Subtract equation (iv) from equation (iii).

$$18x = 126$$
$$x = 7$$

Substitute $x = 7$ into equation (i).

$$42 + 3y = 75$$
$$3y = 33$$
$$y = 11$$

Answer: Oranges cost 7 p each and grapefruit cost 11 p each.

5 oranges and 4 grapefruit cost $(5 \times 7)\,\text{p} + (4 \times 11)\,\text{p}$
$$= (35 + 44)\,\text{p} = 79\,\text{p}.$$

This correct solution would be given full marks.

Incorrect solution

First equation $\quad\quad 3x + 6y = 75 \quad \text{(i)}*$
Second equation $\quad\quad 4x + 5y = 83 \quad \text{(ii)}$

Multiply equation (i) by 5 and equation (ii) by 6.

$$15x + 30y = 375 \quad \text{(iii)}*$$
$$24x + 30y = 498 \quad \text{(iv)}$$

Subtract equation (iii) from equation (iv).

$$9x = 123$$
$$x = 13\tfrac{2}{3}$$

Substitute $x = 13\tfrac{2}{3}$ into equation (i).

$$3(13\tfrac{2}{3}) + 6y = 75$$
$$6y = 34$$
$$y = 5\tfrac{2}{3}$$

Answer: Oranges cost $13\tfrac{2}{3}$ p each and grapefruit cost $5\tfrac{2}{3}$ p each.

5 oranges and 4 grapefruit cost $(5 \times 13\tfrac{2}{3})\,\text{p} + (4 \times 5\tfrac{2}{3})\,\text{p}$
$$= (68\tfrac{1}{3} + 22\tfrac{2}{3})\,\text{p} = 91\,\text{p}$$

This solution is incorrect because of a misreading. Instead of buying 6 oranges and 3 grapefruit to obtain the first equation, 6 grapefruit and 3 oranges were bought. After this error in the first equation, the method and all the subsequent working are correct. However the misreading has led to more complicated arithmetic and has consumed more time in the examination. This is in addition to the loss of marks.

Working omitted or crossed out

At the beginning of this chapter, it was pointed out that a correct answer obtained by a sound method will be given full marks. It has also been demonstrated that marks can be obtained from an incorrect solution provided that the method is correct. However it must be stressed that, if your answer is wrong, the marks for method can only be awarded if your method is clear and this can be judged only if your working is clearly presented.

This does not mean that you can't do simple calculations mentally or that you should write down working unnecessarily. But if you do find it necessary to write working down then it must be part of your solution and not done on scraps of paper.

This also applies to work crossed out. If you think you have made a mistake, then you should cross it out and replace it with the correct work. But work should not be crossed out unless it is definitely going to be replaced. And work should not be crossed out if it is part of your solution. Remember that the work you cross out may be worth some marks for method, even it if does not lead to a correct answer or to any answer!

Finally, if it is necessary to cross out, then do it neatly. Don't obliterate it and don't use eradicator.

Remember that an examiner cannot read what is in your mind, only what is on your paper. Consequently there is a need to present a solution in which the method can clearly be followed. The next two examples are chosen to illustrate these points.

PAPER 1, QUESTION 14 *See page 49.*

Correct solution

Circumference of flower bed is $2\pi r$

$$= 2 \times 3.14 \times 5 \text{ metres}$$
$$= 31.4 \text{ m}$$
$$= 3140 \text{ cm}$$

Number of bulbs is $3140 \div 20 = 157$

Answer: 157 bulbs are planted.

Incorrect solution

Circumference of flower bed is $2\pi r$

$$= 2 \times 3.14 \times 5 \text{ metres}$$
$$= 31.4 \text{ m}$$
$$= 314 \text{ cm*}$$

Number of bulbs is $314 \div 20 = 15.7$
or 16 (to nearest whole number)

Answer: 16 bulbs are planted.

This solution is incorrect and the reason for this is clear. The error occurred when the 31.4 metres was converted to centimetres.
Assuming the marking scheme was:

M1 for substituting into $C = 2\pi r$,
M1 for dividing by 20,
M1 for correct use of units,
A1 for correct answer,

then the first two of these marks would be gained.
But suppose this candidate had not presented all the working but had simply given the answer as 16. Since there would have been no way of knowing how this had been obtained no marks could be given.

PAPER 3, QUESTION 6 *See page 57.*

Correct solution

			£
1 January	1980	Initial amount	500
31 December	1980	Interest	40
			540
1 January	1981	Invested	500
2 January	1981	Total	1040
31 December	1981	Interest	83.20
2 January	1982	Total	1123.20

Answer: (a) Amount on 2 January 1981 is £1040.
(b) Amount on 2 January 1982 is £1123.20.

Incorrect solution

			£
1 January	1980	Initial amount	500
31 December	1980	Interest	4*
			504
1 January	1981	Invested	500
2 January	1981	Total	1004
31 December	1981	Interest	8.032*
2 January	1982	Total	1012.032

Answer: (a) Amount on 2 January 1981 is £1004.

(b) Amount on 2 January 1982 is £1012.032.

This solution is incorrect and again a study of the working reveals the error. Instead of adding 8% of the amount in the account on 31 December 1980, 0.8% was added. A similar error was made when adding the interest on 31 December 1981.

Because all the working is shown and it is clear what the error is, it may be possible to give some marks for this solution. However, if the working had not been shown clearly, the incorrect answers would not have revealed anything and as a result no method marks could be given.

Approximating and degrees of accuracy

Accuracy in numerical questions

Many questions in maths involve the use of measurements, and it is important to realise that when measurements are quoted they can never be given exactly. They are always made to a certain degree of accuracy. For example, if a distance between two towns is said to be 31 miles, it must be assumed that this has been measured correct to the nearest mile. Similarly, if the length of a line is given as 8.4 cm, then we assume it has been measured correct to the nearest 0.1 cm. The degree of accuracy used depends on the particular circumstances. This leads to the question: 'To what degree of accuracy should working be given in an examination?'

Most calculators work with eight-digit numbers, but no one would suggest that this degree of accuracy is necessary for most calculations in real life. Books of mathematical tables usually have four-digit numbers, and even these may be too accurate for many purposes.

However, although it is possible to be too accurate when doing a calculation, it is also possible to use numbers which are not sufficiently accurate and this could well lead to a loss of marks.

Many questions specify the degree of accuracy:

'Give your answer correct to 2 decimal places.'
'Give your answer correct to 3 significant figures.'
'Give your answer correct to the nearest 1 p.'

In cases like these, it is important to realise that, if your answer is to be given to this degree of accuracy, then your working must be more accurate. You should not approximate until the *final* stage of the solution.

When questions do not specify any particular degree of accuracy, or if there is any doubt, then a general rule is to work to 4 significant figures.

The following two examples illustrate how marks may be lost by approximating too early.

PAPER 3, QUESTION 9(a) *See page 58.*

Accurate solution

$$\cos A\hat{B}C = \frac{AB}{BC} \qquad \cos 25° = \frac{AB}{70} \qquad 0.9063 = \frac{AB}{70}$$
$$AB = 0.9063 \times 70 = 63.44$$

Answer: The length of AB is 63.4 cm (correct to 1 decimal place).

Note that it is not necessary to work more accurately than this. However, any approximating should be done only at the final stage of the solution, that is after the answer of 63.44 has been obtained. Compare this with the following solution where the approximation is done earlier.

Inaccurate solution

$$\cos A\hat{B}C = \frac{AB}{BC} \qquad \cos 25° = \frac{AB}{70} \qquad 0.9^* = \frac{AB}{70}$$
$$AB = 0.9 \times 70 = 63$$

Answer: The length of AB is 63 cm.

In this solution the cosine of 25° has been approximated to 0.9 and although the final answer is not too unreasonable, working to this crude degree of accuracy is not normally acceptable and would lose marks in the examination.

PAPER 3, QUESTION 9(b) *See page 58.*

Accurate solution

$$\tan x = \frac{45}{120} = 0.375$$
$$x = 20.56°$$

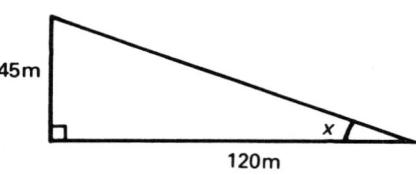
45 m
120 m

Answer: Angle of elevation is 20.56°.

Note that as no degree of accuracy was specified the answer was given correct to 4 significant figures. (The answer given on a calculator is 20.556 045.) Since it seems clear that the original lengths of 120 m and 45 m were measured to 2 significant figures then answers of 20.6° or even 21° are probably sufficiently accurate, but it might be safer to give the answer as 20.56°.

Inaccurate solution

$$\tan x = \frac{45}{120} = 0.4*$$
$$x = 21.8°$$

Answer: Angle of elevation is 21.8°.

In this solution, the decimal 0.375 has been approximated to 0.4. The approximation has been made early in the solution and this has resulted in an incorrect answer. Notice that this is not the same as the answer of 20.6° or 21° obtained by approximating at the very last stage of the accurate solution above. The accuracy mark would not normally be given in this case.

The examples above illustrate how marks may be lost by approximating too early. It is equally important to note that marks may be lost if approximations are not given when they have been asked for in a question.

When an answer is asked to be given correct to 2 decimal places or to 3 significant figures, then the question is testing your knowledge of these terms and marks may be allocated for this particular purpose. The fact that you may have produced a more accurate answer than the one asked for would not prevent you losing accuracy marks. If you do not give the answer to the degree of approximation required, it will be assumed that you do not understand or are unable to carry out the correct approximation.

Accuracy in graphical questions

Some exam questions ask you to draw and interpret graphs, and you are frequently asked to read from your graph. Results read from a graph cannot be as accurate as results obtained from a calculation, but you will be expected to be as accurate as possible. Many graphs are drawn on squared paper with the smallest squares having a side of 2 mm and, when a graph passes through one of these squares, it should be possible to decide whether the line is passing closer to either end or to the middle of the square. In other words you should be able to read your graph to the nearest millimetre. Clearly this will not be possible if your line is very thick or is badly drawn. You can help yourself by ensuring that you have a supply of good pencils with sharp points and a good ruler. When drawing the graph, take care to be as accurate as possible and this also applies when reading from your graph.

Mistakes involving units

Units in the answer

Many answers are not complete unless they are accompanied by the correct units, and marks may be deducted if incorrect units or no units are given. When you write an answer you should ask yourself the following three questions:

Have I given the units?
Are they the correct units?
Are they appropriate units?

Which units are the most appropriate will depend upon the context and the particular measure involved. As a rough guide, the following comments apply.

Length, weight, capacity

These are normally in metric units and the question of which is most appropriate does not arise. Answers of 2.3 km or 2300 m are both correct. Even 2 300 000 mm is correct, but answers involving very large numbers of digits should be avoided, as it is easy to omit a digit and thus lose the accuracy mark. Although these units do not normally cause problems, their careless use can lead to a loss of marks. Writing 2.3 m instead of 2.3 km may be due to an error in your working or it may simply be due to carelessness, but either way it is an incorrect answer and will not be given the accuracy mark.

Money

Answers should normally be given in pounds unless the amount is less than £1. Amounts such as 3758 p should be converted to pounds. The ambiguous use of both £ and p symbols, as for example in £37.58 p, should always be avoided.

Area, volume

Particular care should be taken with these measures, as they frequently lead to errors when giving units. Exam candidates sometimes express areas and volumes in units of length. For example, an area might be given as 32 cm, rather than 32 cm².

Velocity, acceleration

There is often confusion about the units of velocity (speed) and acceleration. Make sure that you understand these units before the exam, and take care to use them correctly when giving answers. If you cannot remember the abbreviations for the units then write them out in full, for example 17 metres per second (velocity) or 17 metres per second per second (acceleration).

Non-decimal units

Most of the measures encountered in exam questions work in the decimal system and conversion between different units is straightforward. For example, 517 mm = 51.7 cm = 0.517 m = 0.000517 km. However, some measures work in non-decimal units and particular care needs to be taken when working with these. One error, which is surprisingly common, occurs when a dot is used to separate units in a non-decimal system. For example, 2 minutes 15 seconds is written as 2.15 minutes. Later the 2.15 is entered into a calculator as a decimal number and it is forgotten that this really represents $2\frac{15}{60}$. For this reason, it is unwise to use a dot to separate units except in the cases where it is being used as a decimal point. The following two examples illustrate this.

PAPER 1, QUESTION 16 *See page 50.*

Correct solution

(a) Average speed is $174 \div 3$.

Answer: Average speed is 58 kilometres per hour.

(b) Distance travelled is $58 \times 2\frac{1}{2}$
$$= 58 \times 2.5$$
$$= 145$$

Answer: Distance travelled is 145 km.

Incorrect solution

(a) Average speed is $174 \div 3$

Answer: Average speed is 58 kilometres per hour.

(b) Distance travelled is $58 \times 2.30^* = 133.4$

Answer: Distance travelled is 133.4 km.

The error is made by thinking of $2\frac{1}{2}$ hours as 2 hours 30 minutes and then writing this as 2.30 hours which is then confused with the decimal number 2.3.

PAPER 2, QUESTION 5(a) *See page 52.*

Correct solution

(a)

Years	Months
13	1
13	7
12	6
11	2
13	5
63	9

Total age is 63 years 9 months.
Average age is found by dividing 63 years 9 months by 5.

Answer: Average age is 12 years 9 months.

Incorrect solution

(a)   Years
                                                                               13.1*
                                                                               13.7
                                                                               12.6
                                                                               11.2
                                                                               13.5
                                                                               ─────
                                                                               64.1*

Average age is found by dividing 64.1 years by 5.

Answer: Average age is 12.82 years.

The error is made when writing 13 years 1 month in the form 13.1 and so on, for each of the ages. The reason for this error is probably not a misunderstanding of how many months there are in a year. It is more likely to be due to careless use of notation. Initially ages such as 13 years 1 month get written in the shortened form 13.1, but later this is forgotten and is treated as the decimal number 13.1.

Inconsistency in use of units

Another common source of error occurs when working is done without sufficient attention being paid to the units in use. For example, an amount £57 in one line of a solution, then appears as 57 p in the next line. Errors such as this are usually due to lack of care. Not only do they lead to an incorrect solution, but also they can lead to an increased amount of work and time in the examination. In the following example we see a typical misuse of units.

PAPER 1, QUESTION 12 *See page 48.*

Correct solution

(a) *Answer:* 3672 units.

(b) 3672 − 2427 = 1245

Answer: 1245 units.

(c) Cost of units is 5.2 p × 1245 = 6474 p
Total amount is £64.74 + £6.50 = £71.24

Answer: Total amount owing is £71.24.

Incorrect solution

(a) *Answer:* 3672 units.

(b) $3672 - 2427 = 1245$

Answer: 1245 units.

(c) Cost of units is $5.2 \times 1245 = 6474$

Total amount is $6474* + 6.50 = 6480.50$

Answer: Total amount owing is £6480.50.

The error arose because insufficient care was being taken to keep note of which units were being used and, as a consequence the 6474 p was assumed to be £6474.

SOME DOS AND DON'TS IN THE EXAMINATION

Do make sure that you have the correct geometrical instruments, sharp pencils and a calculator with a good battery.

Do read a question carefully before you begin the solution.

Do make sure that you copy information from the question paper correctly.

Don't do any working on scrap paper.

Do set out all your working legibly.

Don't cross out working unless it is to be replaced by new work.

Don't use a method of scale drawing if the question asks you to 'calculate'.

Don't use a method of calculation if the question asks you to read the answer from your graph.

Do give answers to the degree of accuracy asked for.

Don't use approximations too early in your solution.

Do try to read from your graphs as accurately as possible.

Do give the correct units with your answer.

Don't use a point to separate units which are non-decimal.

Do be aware of which units you are working in.

SECTION 7
Revising and preparing for the exam

You will probably have finished the syllabus and will have been doing revision exercises at school for many weeks before the exam. In this way your teacher will be trying to ensure that you are fully prepared. However, no teacher can do everything for you, and there is much that you can and must do for yourself. Remember that when you are in the exam room you will be on your own, and you may need to recall any part of the syllabus. It is unlikely that you will be able to remember all the maths you have done unless you have made thorough preparation beforehand. *This means doing adequate revision.* However, before starting you should consider how best to organise your revision as, without careful planning, it is possible to spend time wastefully. A little time at the beginning spent in considering the organisation and techniques of your revision can pay good dividends.

ORGANISING YOUR REVISION

You will need to plan your strategy about six weeks before the exam. Ask yourself: 'When, where and how shall I revise?'

When shall I revise?

First you must make a programme of your revision time. Decide how much time you can afford to spend on mathematics, in relation to the time spent in revising your other subjects. Your allocation will depend partly on the demands of each subject and also on the exam timetable.

Think also about the time of day which is most suitable. Studying maths demands concentration and is probably best done in the early evening. It is more difficult to concentrate later in the evening when your brain is tired.

Remember that although it is important to work hard, it is equally important not to overdo it, so be sensible and allow time for other activities.

Where shall I revise?

Have you got a room in which you can do your work? Although some people seem to be able to work with music in the background, most need an atmosphere of peace and quiet, so choose a room where you will not be disturbed, if possible.

No one is able to concentrate in a room in which the television set is switched on.

Mathematics is a subject which cannot be revised by reading about it. You need to be *doing* it with a pencil and paper. Few people do this satisfactorily in an armchair. Sitting at a desk or table is the best position.

How shall I revise?

Make sure that you know which papers you are being entered for and ask your teacher to show you the syllabus. Compare the material in the syllabus with the appropriate lists in section 3, noting any additional topics.

At first glance there may seem to be a vast amount of work to be done, and it is important not to be overwhelmed by it. You will need to split the work into small amounts, each of which you can set yourself as a target for a session or a group of sessions.

For each revision session, you should have an aim and a clear plan of what you intend to do in that session. This may be to concentrate on a particular part of the syllabus, or it may be to attempt a specified number of questions selected from a revision sheet of examples. Allow yourself a set time to try to achieve your aim, and reward yourself with a break at the end of that time.

Mathematics can only be properly revised by *doing* it. For most of your time this means solving problems. These problems may be from example sheets provided by your teacher, or from past papers, or from papers of specimen questions produced by your examining group. These will help you to get used to the style of questions and the timing of them.

Attempting questions from the specimen papers, or from past papers, or revision sheets, is not only a sensible way to do revision, it is also a good opportunity to practise exam technique. In section 6, it was pointed out that errors are frequently made by misreading the question. Study each question carefully and make sure that you understand exactly what is being asked.

Don't jot down answers in rough. Write out your solutions as you intend to in the exam, neatly and clearly. Read through them afterwards, deciding whether an examiner could follow your argument. Remember that writing a solution to a mathematical problem is not like writing an essay. You can be concise. However you must include all the relevant steps in the argument.

If you have difficulty with a particular question, then you will need to refer to your notes or your text-book. This is the time when you are doing revision in the true sense of the word. Not only must you try to solve your immediate problem, but also you must try to ensure that you don't need to consult your notes again on this particular point. Make a summary of key facts which will help you to recall, then make a genuine effort to learn this material over the next two or three days.

If you have difficulty in understanding a question, even with the help of your text-book, then there are a number of things to try:

1 Read the question again carefully to make sure you have not misread or misinterpreted it.

2 Identify the area of work which is involved, and try to recall whether you have done a similar question in the past.

3 See if the problem can be split up into smaller parts which can be tackled individually. Sometimes a question seems lengthy and involved, when in reality it consists of a number of small straightforward parts.

4 See if it is possible to draw a picture or diagram. This may help you to visualise the problem.

5 Take a break. Do something else in the meantime and come back to the question later. It may be that you need a fresh start at the question.

Finally if you find that you still don't understand, then make a note of your difficulties and ask your teacher.

Consult the syllabus and make a note of facts which you will be required to use. In list 1, these will include the formula for the area of a triangle or the conversion of millimetres to centimetres. Other lists include use of such formulae as the area of a circle or parallelogram, the theorem of Pythagoras, and the sine, cosine and tangent of an angle.

It may not be necessary to learn some of these formulae, as they will be given to you on the question paper; the syllabus will tell you which these are. Others will need to be learned, so make a conscious effort to do this, and test yourself to make sure that you know them perfectly. You will not get much sympathy from examiners, nor method marks, if you confuse sine with cosine or quote Pythagoras incorrectly.

PREPARING FOR THE EXAM

Before the exam, collect all the equipment which you will require. This will probably include:

> two pens, one for emergency;
> two pencils, with sharp points, for diagrams;
> calculator, with good battery;
> ruler, compasses, protractor;
> rubber, pencil sharpener;
> watch, in case you can't see the exam room clock.

Make sure that you understand your calculator. You may not have to use all the buttons, but you must be very familiar with those that you will need. The exam room is not the place to be sorting out calculator buttons.

Look again at past papers or specimen papers, but this time concentrate on the style of the paper. How much time is allowed? How many questions are set? Study the mark allocation for individual questions. Are some questions given many more marks than others? Try to work out an approximate allocation of the available time which you could allow to answer individual questions. For example, a question which carries 10 marks out of a total of 100 should take you about one tenth of the total time allowed.

In the examination itself, it would be wrong to time each question too rigidly, but you must try to pace yourself. If a question is worth 4 marks and you are still writing the solution after ten minutes, then you have probably made an error and your time would be better spent doing another question. Are some questions easier than others? It is often a good idea to tackle these first, as this should give you confidence. You can then return to the more difficult ones later on.

Finally refer again to the list of dos and don'ts at the end of section 6, and remember that neat work often means accurate work.

We hope you have found this book helpful. Good luck in the examination!

NB Assessment patterns are compared in the table overleaf.

A comparison of assessment patterns

		SEG	NEA
MARKS	Course:	40	25
	Exam:	50	75
	Other:	Aural 14	
PAPERS (All have three levels)		Sit 2 papers from a chain of 4. Level 1: Grades E – G Level 2: Grades C – F Level 3: Grades A – D Aural: 2 from a chain of 4.	Sit 2 papers from a chain of 4. Level P: Grades E – G Level Q: Grades C – F* Level R: Grades A – D* * Lower grades awarded in exceptional circumstances.
COURSEWORK ASSIGNMENTS		3 Units of work One must be an 'extended piece'. Other two are 'single tasks' or a series of short assignments.	Centres are responsible for deciding nature of coursework 'The length of a piece of work may vary from a few minutes' activity to work pursued over several weeks'.
BOARD PRESCRIPTION AND GUIDANCE ON TASK CHOICE		'The provision of suitable activities is left to the teacher'. Together the units should involve all of the following selection: Data handling, problem solving, interpretations and generalisations of results, communication of results.	A list of possible activities is offered only as a guide. 'Teachers are free to devise their own assignments.'
ALLOCATION OF MARKS		Extended piece: 12 × 4 (weighting) 2 other units each: 12 × 2 (weighting) Oral aspect: 12 × 2 (weighting) Total: 120 scaled to 40	Practical work: 30 Investigation: 40 Assimilation: 30 Total: 100 scaled to 25
BOARD PRESCRIPTION AND GUIDANCE ON MARKING		4 pages of questions to ask either about the work or the pupil are offered as guidance. The teachers' aim is to award a grade first and numerical mark afterwards. Detailed cumulative grade descriptions are given.	Assessment guide outlines the main points a teacher should consider and the mark ranges which can be used. These include: Planning 0–12 Skills of using equipment 0– 6 Understanding of equipment 0–12 Clarity and conciseness of expression 0–10 Recall of knowledge 0– 3 Understanding of concepts and subject matter involved 0–10
MODERATION		Consortium consensus or by inspection by the board.	Statistically against written paper marks, but poor coursework cannot affect grades adversely (1988–91).

MEG	LEAG	WJEC
25	25	22.2
75	70	74.1
	Mental 5	Aural 3.7

MEG	LEAG	WJEC
3 different pairs of papers Foundation Grades E – G Intermediate Grades C – F Higher: Grades A – D	Sit 2 papers from a chain of 4 Level X: Grades E – G Level Y: Grades C – F Level Z: Grades A – D Mental: 3 different tests	Sit 2 papers from a chain of 4 Level 1: Grades E – G Level 2: Grades C – F Level 3: Grades A – D Aural: 1 test for Levels 2 and 3, separate test for Level 1.
5 Assignments, each 2–3 weeks work One from each of: Practical Geometry Everyday Applications Statistics/Probability Investigations Centre approved topic	5 Investigations. One or two from each of: Pure Investigation Problems Practical work	Level 1: An investigation of a particular theme using various mathematical techniques and three exercises demonstrating application of certain practical skills. Levels 2 and 3: A practical investigation and a problem solving investigation
Topics are suggested for each of the task headings, but 'candidates are encouraged to select suitable topics outside this list.'	7 coursework tasks/investigations will be set by the board. Candidates may submit investigations of their own choice provided they fall into the required 3 categories.	A choice of 2 topics for each task at Levels 2 and 3 will be set. 2 topics and 4 exercises will be set for Level 1. Centres may choose their own topics provided they are of similar standard to those of the board

For each task there are 4 marks
for each of:
Design/Strategy
Maths content
Accuracy
Presentation and Clarity
of Argument
A Controlled Element (brief
text or oral exchange)
 	
Total: 20 x 5 = 100 scaled to 25
	Each task marked out of:
	7 Strategy
	7 Implementation and Reasoning
	6 Interpretation and
	Communication
	
	Total: 20 x 5 = 100 scaled to 25
		The marks are divided between:
		(i) The finished assignment.
		    Understanding 3
		    Strategy 5
		    Content and Development 6
		    Communication 7
		(ii) Continuous assessment including
		    oral assessment.
		    Understanding 3
		    Method 3
		    Conclusion 3
		Total: 30 x 2 scaled to 22.2

The criteria for awarding 4, 2 and 0 marks for each section of each task are given.	The criteria for awarding 2, 5 and 7 marks for Strategy and Implementation and 1, 4 and 6 for Interpretation are given.	A description of the meaning of each of the headings is followed by the criteria for awarding each individual mark.
A random sample by board's Assessors.	A random sample by board's Moderators.	Consortium moderation or by inspection by the board.

% MARKS – Course:	20
Exam:	70
Other:	Award for computation test 10

PAPERS	3 different pairs of papers
	Basic: Grades: E – G
	Intermediate: Grades: C – F
	High: Grades: A – D

| COURSEWORK ASSIGNMENTS | 4 assignments (One extended piece of work may count as two). At least one from each of the two areas: |

1. Practical geometry/Measurement/ Everyday applications/Statistical work.
2. Pure Mathematics Investigations.

| BOARD PRESCRIPTION AND GUIDANCE ON TASK CHOICE | 'Teachers are responsible for devising the assignments'. The total assessed work should cover opportunities to: |

a. organise and interpret information;
b. collect and select data/measurements;
c. select and carry out appropriate calculations;
d. organise and solve problems;
e. check, interpret and evaluate results;
f. recognise patterns, propose generalisations (and explore their validity);
g. explain methods/strategies adopted.

'It is essential that candidates be set tasks which will enable them to demonstrate what they know, understand and can do.' Teachers should select only assignments which are within the capabilities of the particular candidate. Group assignments are permitted if individual contributions can be reliably assessed.

ALLOCATION OF MARKS		Basic	Int.	High
	Comprehension of task and planning:	3	5	7
	Examination of task:	3	5	7
	Communication and Evaluation:	3	5	7
	Maximum possible: (each scaled to 20%)	36	60	84

BOARD PRESCRIPTION AND GUIDANCE ON MARKING	Candidates are expected to do no more than four assignments altogether and teachers will select for formal assessment those likely to obtain the highest marks. General guidelines are given in the form of descriptions of the three categories for marks, but 'teachers will be required to attend training workshops organised by the Council at which they will be given detailed information regarding the assessment of assignments'.
MODERATION	Moderation by the Council's Coursework Moderator.